Identity Authentication and Authorization

James Relington

DEDICATION

This book is dedicated to all the professionals working tirelessly to secure digital identities and protect organizations from ever-evolving threats. To the cybersecurity teams, IT administrators, and identity management experts who ensure safe and seamless access for users—your work is invaluable. And to my family and friends, whose support and encouragement made this journey possible, thank you.

AKNOWLEDGEMENTS

I would like to express my deepest gratitude to everyone who contributed to the creation of this book. To my colleagues and mentors in the cybersecurity and identity management field, your insights and expertise have been invaluable. To the organizations and professionals who shared their experiences and best practices, your contributions have enriched this work. A special thanks to my family and friends for their unwavering support and encouragement throughout this journey. Finally, to the readers, thank you for your interest in identity lifecycle management—may this book help you navigate the evolving landscape of digital security with confidence.

The Foundation of Digital Identity

Security In today's interconnected world, digital identity has become an essential pillar supporting the framework of modern society. From accessing personal email accounts to conducting high-stakes financial transactions, the concept of identity in the digital realm underpins almost every online interaction. But what exactly is digital identity, and why has it become so pivotal in our daily lives?

At its core, digital identity refers to the unique set of attributes and credentials that represent an individual, organization, or device within digital ecosystems. This collection of data can include anything from usernames and passwords to biometric data like fingerprints or facial recognition patterns. Even metadata such as IP addresses, browsing habits, and device IDs contribute to this complex, evolving digital persona. Unlike physical identity, which relies on tangible proof like driver's licenses or passports, digital identity is intangible, dynamic, and susceptible to constant change as new data points are added with every interaction.

The concept of digital identity emerged with the proliferation of the internet in the late 20th century. As people began to spend more time online, engaging in activities ranging from social networking to e-commerce, the need for secure, reliable methods of identifying users became apparent. Initially, simple usernames and passwords sufficed to establish identity. However, as cyber threats grew more sophisticated and the value of online data skyrocketed, it became clear that more robust systems were required to ensure both the security and privacy of digital interactions.

The foundation of digital identity is built upon two interrelated concepts: authentication and authorization. Authentication is the process of verifying that a user is who they claim to be. This might involve entering a password, providing a fingerprint, or responding to a security question. Once authentication is successfully completed, authorization comes into play. Authorization determines what resources or information the authenticated user has permission to access. For instance, after logging into a bank account (authentication), a user might be authorized to view their account balance but not to modify administrative settings reserved for bank employees.

Central to this framework is the concept of trust. In the digital world, trust is not established through face-to-face interactions but rather through the integrity of the systems that manage digital identities. Identity providers (IdPs) play a crucial role in this ecosystem by managing and verifying the identities of users. These can be standalone organizations like Google or Facebook, which offer social login options, or enterprise solutions that provide secure identity management for businesses. Trust in these providers is paramount; if an identity provider is compromised, the ripple effects can be devastating, leading to data breaches, financial loss, and erosion of user confidence.

The evolution of digital identity has been marked by a shift from centralized to decentralized systems. Traditionally, identity data was stored and managed by a single entity, such as a government agency or a corporation. While this model offers simplicity, it also creates a single point of failure. If the central repository is hacked or mismanaged, all the identities it contains are at risk. Decentralized identity systems aim to mitigate this risk by distributing identity data across multiple nodes, often using blockchain technology to ensure security and immutability. This model empowers individuals by giving them greater control over their identity data, reducing reliance on centralized authorities.

As digital identity systems have grown more sophisticated, so too have the threats they face. Identity theft, phishing attacks, and data breaches are common tactics employed by cybercriminals to exploit vulnerabilities in identity management systems. The consequences of a compromised digital identity can be severe, ranging from unauthorized access to sensitive information to financial fraud and reputational damage. To combat these threats, organizations have adopted multi-factor authentication (MFA) strategies, which require users to provide multiple forms of verification before granting access. This could involve something the user knows (a password), something the user has (a security token), and something the user is (biometric data).

The rise of biometric authentication represents a significant milestone in the evolution of digital identity. Unlike traditional methods, which rely on knowledge or possessions that can be stolen or forgotten, biometric authentication uses unique physical characteristics that are difficult to replicate. Fingerprints, facial recognition, iris scans, and even voice patterns are increasingly used to verify identity with a high degree of accuracy. However, the adoption of biometrics also raises concerns about privacy and data security. Unlike passwords, biometric data cannot be easily changed if compromised, making it a prime target for cybercriminals.

In parallel with technological advancements, the legal and regulatory landscape surrounding digital identity has also evolved. Governments and international bodies have introduced legislation aimed at protecting personal data and ensuring the secure management of digital identities. Regulations such as the General Data Protection Regulation (GDPR) in the European Union and the California Consumer Privacy Act (CCPA) in the United States impose strict requirements on how organizations collect, store, and process identity data. These laws emphasize the importance of user consent, data minimization, and transparency, forcing organizations to adopt more stringent security measures and to be more accountable for the protection of digital identities.

The importance of digital identity extends beyond individual users and organizations to encompass broader societal implications. As governments digitize public services and businesses shift to online models, the ability to establish and verify digital identities becomes critical to ensuring equal access to resources and opportunities. Digital identity plays a vital role in areas such as healthcare, education, and financial inclusion, enabling people to access essential services, prove their credentials, and participate fully in the digital economy. For marginalized communities and those in developing regions, digital identity can be a powerful tool for empowerment, providing a means to access services and opportunities that might otherwise be out of reach.

However, the widespread adoption of digital identity systems also brings ethical considerations to the forefront. Issues of surveillance, data privacy, and the potential for misuse of identity data pose significant challenges. There is an ongoing debate about the balance between security and privacy, as well as the role of governments and corporations in managing digital identities. Ensuring that digital identity systems are designed with transparency, fairness, and respect for individual rights is essential to building trust and fostering a secure digital environment.

Looking ahead, the future of digital identity is likely to be shaped by emerging technologies such as artificial intelligence, machine learning, and blockchain. These technologies have the potential to enhance the security, efficiency, and user experience of identity systems, while also addressing some of the current challenges related to privacy and data control. As the digital landscape continues to evolve, the foundation of digital identity will remain a critical component of the infrastructure that supports our increasingly connected world. The ability to securely and reliably establish identity in the digital realm is not just a technical necessity—it is a cornerstone of modern society, enabling trust, facilitating innovation, and protecting the fundamental rights of individuals in the digital age.

Authentication vs. Authorization: Understanding the Difference

In the realm of digital security, two concepts often appear together, yet they serve fundamentally different purposes: authentication and authorization. While they are closely linked in managing access to systems and resources, understanding the distinction between them is critical for anyone involved in IT, cybersecurity, or even regular users navigating digital environments. Confusing these two can lead to security vulnerabilities, misconfigurations, and a false sense of protection. By exploring what each term means, how they interact, and why they matter, we can gain a clearer picture of how digital security frameworks operate.

Authentication is the process of verifying an individual's identity. It answers a simple but vital question: Are you who you claim to be? When you log into an email account, swipe your fingerprint on a smartphone, or enter a PIN at an ATM, you are engaging in authentication. The goal is to ensure that the person attempting to gain access is indeed the rightful owner of the credentials or device. Authentication can take many forms, ranging from traditional methods like usernames and passwords to more advanced techniques like biometric scans, hardware tokens, or multi-factor authentication (MFA).

Multi-factor authentication has become especially important in recent years due to the increasing sophistication of cyberattacks. Instead of relying on a single form of verification, MFA requires users to provide multiple credentials from different categories: something they know (like a password), something they have (like a smartphone or a security token), and something they are (like a fingerprint or facial recognition). By combining these elements, MFA significantly reduces the likelihood of unauthorized access, even if one factor—such as a password—is compromised.

However, authentication alone doesn't dictate what a user can do once they've been verified. This is where authorization comes into play. Authorization determines what an authenticated user is allowed to access and what actions they can perform within a system. While authentication answers the question of identity, authorization addresses the issue of permissions. For instance, after logging into a corporate network, an employee might be authenticated, but their authorization will dictate whether they can access sensitive financial records, modify company data, or simply view general information.

The relationship between authentication and authorization can be compared to checking into a hotel. When you arrive at the front desk, the receptionist asks for your identification and booking confirmation. This is the authentication step—verifying that you are the person who made the reservation. Once authenticated, you receive a key card that grants access to your room and perhaps certain common areas like the gym or pool. However, that same key card won't grant you access to other guests' rooms or restricted staff areas. The limitations placed on your access reflect the authorization process.

Despite their clear differences, authentication and authorization are often implemented together in security systems, creating a layered defense strategy. For example, when logging into an online banking application, the system first authenticates your identity using a password or biometric scan. Once authenticated, the system checks your authorization to determine which accounts you can view, whether you can initiate transfers, or if you have administrative privileges to modify account settings. Without both processes working in tandem, the security of the system would be incomplete.

One of the key reasons these concepts are frequently confused is that they often occur sequentially, giving the impression that they are the same process. Yet, understanding their separation is critical in both designing secure systems and troubleshooting access issues. For instance, if a user reports that they can log into a system but cannot access specific files or features, the problem likely lies in the authorization settings, not authentication. Conversely, if they are unable to log in at all, the issue is probably related to authentication.

Different technologies and protocols manage authentication and authorization, each designed to address specific needs within digital ecosystems. Authentication protocols like LDAP (Lightweight Directory Access Protocol) and Kerberos focus on verifying user identities, while authorization frameworks like OAuth and role-based access control (RBAC) manage permissions and resource access. OAuth, for instance, allows users to grant third-party applications limited access to their data without sharing their passwords, a common feature seen when logging into new services using Google or Facebook credentials. This division of responsibilities between protocols further underscores the distinction between authentication and authorization.

Another crucial aspect to consider is how these processes are managed in modern, cloud-based environments. In traditional on-premises systems, authentication and authorization might be handled by the same server or directory service. However, with the shift to cloud computing and distributed systems, these functions are often separated across different platforms and services. Identity providers (IdPs) like Okta or Microsoft Azure Active Directory may handle authentication, while separate systems or applications manage authorization. This decoupling adds complexity but also offers greater flexibility and scalability, allowing organizations to tailor access controls to meet specific security requirements.

The rise of decentralized identity systems adds another layer of complexity to this dynamic. In decentralized models, individuals have greater control over their identity data, often using blockchain technology to verify credentials without relying on a central authority. Authentication in these systems focuses on proving ownership of cryptographic keys, while authorization can be managed through smart contracts that define access rules in an immutable, transparent way. This shift represents a significant departure from traditional identity management, highlighting the evolving nature of how authentication and authorization are implemented.

While both processes are essential for securing digital systems, they also raise important ethical and privacy considerations. Overly stringent authentication methods can create barriers to access, particularly for marginalized communities or individuals with limited access to technology. At the same time, poorly managed authorization systems can lead to over-permissioned accounts, where users have more access than necessary, increasing the risk of data breaches or internal threats. Striking the right balance between security and usability is an ongoing challenge for organizations and developers.

Furthermore, the principles of least privilege and need-to-know are central to effective authorization. These principles dictate that users should only have access to the resources necessary for their roles and nothing more. Implementing these principles requires regular audits and reviews of access permissions to ensure that they align with current roles and responsibilities. Failing to do so can result in privilege creep, where users accumulate access rights over time, potentially exposing sensitive data to unnecessary risk.

As cyber threats continue to evolve, so too must our approaches to authentication and authorization. Emerging technologies like artificial intelligence and machine learning are being integrated into identity and access management systems to detect unusual behavior and adapt access controls in real-time. For example, a system might flag an authentication attempt from an unusual location or deny authorization for a transaction that deviates from a user's typical behavior patterns. These advancements offer promising ways to enhance security without compromising user experience.

In sum, understanding the difference between authentication and authorization is fundamental to building secure digital systems. While authentication verifies identity, authorization governs access, and both must work together to protect sensitive information and resources. As technology continues to advance and digital interactions become increasingly complex, the ability to effectively manage authentication and authorization will remain a cornerstone of cybersecurity and digital trust.

The Evolution of Identity Management Systems

The story of identity management systems is closely tied to the rapid growth of technology and the increasing need for secure digital interactions. In the early days of computing, identity management was a simple concept. Users were identified by unique usernames and authenticated through passwords stored on local systems. These rudimentary setups were sufficient when computer networks were isolated and relatively small. However, as technology advanced and networks became interconnected, the limitations of these basic systems became apparent, paving the way for the evolution of more sophisticated identity management solutions.

In the 1960s and 1970s, the first multi-user systems emerged, primarily within academic and governmental institutions. These early systems required basic forms of identity management to differentiate between users accessing the same mainframe. Usernames and passwords were stored in simple text files, often without encryption, reflecting a time when security threats were minimal, and trust within closed networks was high. The concept of access control was limited to ensuring that users could access only their own files, with little thought given to broader security implications.

As the 1980s approached, the rise of personal computers and local area networks (LANs) introduced new challenges. Organizations began to deploy more computers connected within internal networks, necessitating centralized management of user identities. This era saw the introduction of directory services like the Lightweight Directory Access Protocol (LDAP), which allowed organizations to store and manage user credentials in a centralized database. LDAP provided a standardized method for querying and modifying directory information, laying the groundwork for more scalable identity management systems. Despite these advancements, security remained relatively simple, with usernames and passwords still serving as the primary means of authentication.

The explosion of the internet in the 1990s marked a turning point in the evolution of identity management systems. With the web connecting millions of users and systems globally, the need for more robust and scalable identity solutions became urgent. Passwords, once sufficient for isolated systems, proved inadequate in an environment where phishing attacks, credential theft, and unauthorized access became common threats. To address these challenges, organizations began implementing more complex identity management frameworks, incorporating multi-factor authentication, single sign-on (SSO), and federated identity systems.

Single sign-on emerged as a critical innovation during this period, allowing users to authenticate once and gain access to multiple applications and services without repeatedly entering credentials. This not only improved user experience but also reduced the risk of password fatigue, where users resorted to weak or reused passwords across different systems. SSO solutions like Kerberos provided secure authentication mechanisms for enterprise environments, while web-based SSO protocols like SAML (Security Assertion Markup Language) enabled seamless access across different web applications.

Federated identity systems further advanced the concept of cross-domain authentication by allowing users to use credentials from one organization to access resources in another. This was particularly useful in business-to-business (B2B) environments, where companies needed to collaborate securely without managing separate identities for each partner. Standards like SAML and later OAuth facilitated this interoperability, enabling users to log into third-party applications using credentials from trusted identity providers like Google, Microsoft, or Facebook.

The 2000s witnessed the rise of cloud computing, which introduced new complexities to identity management. With organizations moving their applications and data to the cloud, traditional on-premises identity management systems struggled to keep up. The need for identity solutions that could span both on-premises and cloud environments led to the development of hybrid identity management systems. These systems combined local directory services with cloud-based identity providers, enabling organizations to manage user identities consistently across diverse environments.

Identity as a Service (IDaaS) emerged as a response to the growing demand for cloud-based identity solutions. IDaaS platforms like Okta, Microsoft Azure Active Directory, and Ping Identity provided scalable, flexible identity management services that could integrate with a wide range of cloud applications. These platforms offered features like SSO, multi-factor authentication, and identity governance, allowing organizations to centralize their identity management efforts while leveraging the benefits of the cloud. The shift to IDaaS also reflected a broader trend towards outsourcing non-core IT functions to specialized providers, enabling organizations to focus on their core business activities while ensuring robust identity security.

The increasing complexity of identity management systems also brought greater attention to identity governance and administration (IGA). IGA focuses on ensuring that the right individuals have access to the right resources at the right times for the right reasons. This involves not only managing user identities and permissions but also auditing and reporting on access activities to ensure compliance with regulatory requirements. The introduction of regulations like the General Data Protection Regulation (GDPR) and the California Consumer Privacy Act (CCPA) further emphasized the importance of robust identity governance, requiring organizations to implement strict controls over personal data and access rights.

As the 2010s progressed, the rise of mobile devices and the Internet of Things (IoT) added new dimensions to identity management. With users accessing applications and services from a growing array of devices, identity management systems needed to accommodate device-based authentication and ensure secure access across heterogeneous environments. This led to the development of adaptive authentication techniques, which assess the risk of an authentication attempt based on factors like device type, location, and user behavior.

By incorporating contextual information, adaptive authentication systems could provide stronger security while maintaining a seamless user experience.

Another significant development during this period was the shift towards passwordless authentication. Recognizing the inherent weaknesses of passwords, organizations began exploring alternative methods of authentication that rely on biometrics, cryptographic keys, and other factors. Biometric authentication, such as fingerprint scanning and facial recognition, became increasingly common in consumer devices, while enterprises adopted solutions like FIDO2 and WebAuthn to enable secure, passwordless access to applications and systems.

Decentralized identity represents the latest frontier in the evolution of identity management systems. Unlike traditional models, where identity data is stored and managed by centralized authorities, decentralized identity systems give individuals greater control over their own identities. Using blockchain technology and cryptographic proofs, these systems allow users to manage and share their identity data securely without relying on a central authority. Self-sovereign identity (SSI) is a key concept in this space, emphasizing the individual's ownership and control over their digital identity. Decentralized identity holds the potential to transform how identities are managed, reducing the risk of data breaches and enhancing privacy.

Throughout this evolution, the role of identity management has expanded beyond simply granting access to systems and applications. It has become a critical component of cybersecurity, regulatory compliance, and digital trust. As technology continues to advance and the digital landscape grows increasingly complex, identity management systems will need to evolve in parallel, incorporating new technologies and addressing emerging challenges. The journey from simple usernames and passwords to sophisticated, decentralized identity frameworks reflects the ongoing quest to balance security, usability, and privacy in an ever-changing digital world.

Multi-Factor Authentication: Strengthening Security Layers

As the digital world continues to expand, so too do the risks associated with unauthorized access and cybercrime. Passwords, once considered the cornerstone of online security, have proven increasingly vulnerable to attacks such as phishing, credential stuffing, and brute-force attempts. The growing sophistication of cyber threats has highlighted the need for stronger, more resilient methods of protecting sensitive information. Multi-Factor Authentication (MFA) has emerged as one of the most effective tools for strengthening security layers, offering a robust defense against unauthorized access by requiring users to verify their identity through multiple factors.

At its core, Multi-Factor Authentication operates on a simple but powerful principle: instead of relying solely on a single form of verification, such as a password, users must provide additional credentials from different categories. These categories typically include something the user knows (a password or PIN), something the user has (a physical device like a smartphone or hardware token), and something the user is (biometric data like fingerprints or facial recognition). By combining these distinct factors, MFA creates multiple barriers that an attacker must overcome, significantly reducing the likelihood of a successful breach.

The weaknesses of single-factor authentication, particularly passwords, have been well-documented over the years. Despite repeated warnings and security campaigns, many users continue to rely on weak, easily guessable passwords or reuse the same credentials across multiple platforms. This behavior opens the door to a range of attacks, from simple guessing to more sophisticated techniques like phishing, where attackers trick users into revealing their login information. Even complex passwords are vulnerable if stored improperly or exposed through data breaches. Multi-Factor Authentication addresses these vulnerabilities by ensuring that even if one factor is compromised, an attacker would still need to bypass additional layers of security.

One of the most common forms of MFA involves the use of one-time passwords (OTPs) sent to a user's mobile device via SMS or generated through an authenticator app. After entering their regular password, the user must input the OTP to complete the login process. While this method is relatively simple to implement and offers a significant improvement over single-factor authentication, it is not without its vulnerabilities. SMS-based OTPs, for instance, can be intercepted through SIM-swapping attacks or compromised mobile networks. Recognizing these risks, many organizations have shifted towards more secure methods, such as app-based OTPs or push notifications that require users to approve login attempts directly from their devices.

Hardware tokens represent another widely used MFA method, particularly in high-security environments. These physical devices generate time-sensitive codes that must be entered during the login process. Because hardware tokens are not connected to the internet, they are immune to many common cyber threats, such as phishing or malware. However, they come with their own set of challenges, including the risk of loss, theft, or damage. Additionally, distributing and managing hardware tokens can be logistically complex and costly, especially for large organizations with thousands of users.

Biometric authentication has gained significant traction in recent years as a convenient and secure form of MFA. By leveraging unique physical characteristics, such as fingerprints, facial recognition, or iris scans, biometric authentication offers a high level of security with minimal user effort. Unlike passwords or tokens, biometric traits are difficult to replicate, providing a strong deterrent against unauthorized access. However, biometrics also raise important privacy and security concerns. Unlike passwords, biometric data cannot be easily changed if compromised. A stolen fingerprint or facial scan could have long-lasting implications, especially if the data is stored insecurely or used across multiple systems.

The implementation of MFA extends beyond protecting individual user accounts; it plays a critical role in securing entire organizations and digital ecosystems. In corporate environments, MFA helps safeguard sensitive data, intellectual property, and critical systems from both external threats and insider risks. By requiring multiple forms of verification, organizations can enforce stricter access controls, ensuring that only authorized personnel can access specific resources. This is particularly important in industries like finance, healthcare, and government, where the consequences of unauthorized access can be severe.

Despite its clear benefits, the adoption of MFA has not been universal. Many organizations and individuals hesitate to implement MFA due to concerns about user experience, cost, and complexity. Some users find the additional steps cumbersome, particularly if they need to authenticate frequently throughout the day. For organizations, integrating MFA into existing systems can require significant time and resources, especially if legacy applications are involved. However, the growing availability of user-friendly MFA solutions and the increasing awareness of cyber threats have helped to mitigate these concerns, leading to wider adoption across industries.

The rise of adaptive or risk-based authentication represents an evolution of traditional MFA. Instead of applying the same authentication requirements in every situation, adaptive authentication assesses the risk of each login attempt based on contextual factors, such as the user's location, device, or behavior. For example, if a user logs in from a trusted device in their usual location, the system might only require a password. However, if the same user attempts to log in from an unfamiliar location or device, the system could prompt for additional verification, such as a biometric scan or OTP. This approach balances security with user convenience, reducing friction for legitimate users while maintaining strong defenses against suspicious activity.

Cloud computing and the proliferation of remote work have further highlighted the importance of MFA in today's digital landscape. As employees access corporate resources from various locations and devices, the traditional network perimeter has all but disappeared. MFA provides a critical layer of security in this environment, ensuring that access to sensitive data and systems is tightly controlled regardless of where users are located. Many cloud service providers, such as Microsoft Azure, Amazon Web Services, and Google Cloud, have integrated MFA into their platforms, enabling organizations to enforce strong authentication policies across their cloud environments.

Regulatory requirements have also driven the adoption of MFA in many sectors. Laws and standards such as the General Data Protection Regulation (GDPR), the Payment Card Industry Data Security Standard (PCI DSS), and the Health Insurance Portability and Accountability Act (HIPAA) mandate strong authentication measures to protect sensitive data. Failure to comply with these regulations can result in significant financial penalties and reputational damage, providing organizations with a compelling incentive to implement MFA. Furthermore, insurers increasingly view MFA as a critical component of cybersecurity hygiene, with some offering better terms or reduced premiums to organizations that deploy robust authentication measures.

The future of Multi-Factor Authentication is likely to be shaped by emerging technologies and evolving security threats. Passwordless authentication, for example, represents a natural progression from traditional MFA, eliminating the weakest link—passwords—entirely. Solutions like FIDO2 and WebAuthn leverage public-key cryptography to provide secure, password-free authentication, often combined with biometrics or hardware tokens. As these technologies mature, they promise to deliver even stronger security with a more seamless user experience.

Artificial intelligence and machine learning are also poised to play a role in the future of MFA. By analyzing user behavior and identifying anomalies in real-time, AI-driven systems can enhance adaptive authentication, dynamically adjusting security requirements based on the perceived risk of each interaction. This approach not only strengthens security but also minimizes the impact on legitimate users, allowing for a more intuitive and responsive authentication process.

Multi-Factor Authentication has proven to be an essential tool in the fight against cybercrime, offering a powerful defense against unauthorized access and data breaches. While no security measure is foolproof, the layered protection provided by MFA significantly raises the bar for attackers, making it one of the most effective strategies in modern cybersecurity. As technology continues to evolve and new threats emerge, MFA will remain a cornerstone of digital security, adapting to meet the needs of an increasingly connected world.

Single Sign-On (SSO) and Seamless Access

In today's digital landscape, users interact with countless applications, platforms, and services daily, each typically requiring its own set of login credentials. This growing complexity has led to password fatigue, where users are overwhelmed by the need to remember multiple usernames and passwords. In response to this challenge, Single Sign-On (SSO) has emerged as a pivotal solution, offering a way to streamline authentication processes while enhancing security. By allowing users to access multiple applications with a single set of credentials, SSO simplifies the user experience and reduces the risks associated with poor password management.

Single Sign-On is an authentication process that enables a user to log in once and gain access to multiple systems without being prompted to log in again at each of them. The core idea behind SSO is to create a centralized authentication mechanism that maintains secure communication between various applications and services. This approach not only makes life easier for users, who no longer need to remember numerous passwords, but it also reduces the administrative burden on IT departments tasked with managing user credentials across disparate systems.

The technical foundation of SSO lies in trust relationships between an identity provider (IdP) and service providers (SPs). The identity provider is responsible for authenticating the user and issuing an authentication token, which is then used to gain access to the service providers' applications. These tokens typically include encrypted information about the user's identity and permissions, allowing service providers to verify the user's credentials without requiring direct access to sensitive authentication data. This process ensures that the user's login credentials are handled securely, minimizing the risk of credential theft or exposure.

One of the most common protocols used to implement SSO is the Security Assertion Markup Language (SAML). SAML is an XML-based standard that facilitates the exchange of authentication and authorization data between the identity provider and service providers. When a user attempts to access a service, the service provider redirects them to the identity provider for authentication. Once authenticated, the identity provider sends a SAML assertion back to the service provider, granting the user access. This seamless flow allows users to move between different services without the need to repeatedly enter their credentials.

Another widely used SSO protocol is OAuth, particularly when combined with OpenID Connect (OIDC). While OAuth is primarily an authorization framework, it can be extended to handle authentication when paired with OIDC. This combination is commonly used in web and mobile applications, where users can log in using their credentials from trusted platforms like Google, Facebook, or Microsoft. By leveraging these existing credentials, users can quickly and securely access new applications without the need to create and manage additional accounts.

The benefits of Single Sign-On extend beyond convenience. By centralizing the authentication process, SSO significantly enhances security. One of the primary security advantages is the reduction in password-related vulnerabilities. Since users only need to remember and manage a single set of credentials, they are less likely to resort to insecure practices like using weak passwords, reusing passwords across multiple sites, or writing them down. Additionally, organizations can enforce stronger password policies, multi-factor authentication (MFA), and other security measures more consistently when managing a single point of authentication.

SSO also simplifies the process of onboarding and offboarding employees within organizations. When a new employee joins, IT administrators can quickly grant access to all necessary applications through the centralized identity provider. Conversely, when an employee leaves the organization, disabling their access to the identity provider automatically revokes their access to all connected services. This streamlined approach reduces the risk of orphaned accounts—accounts that remain active after an employee has left—which are a common target for malicious actors.

However, while SSO offers numerous advantages, it is not without its challenges and risks. The most significant risk associated with SSO is the potential for a single point of failure. Since all authentication relies on the identity provider, a compromise of this central system can grant attackers access to all connected applications and services. To mitigate this risk, organizations must implement robust security measures, such as strong encryption, multi-factor authentication, and continuous monitoring for suspicious activity.

Another challenge is the complexity of integrating SSO into existing systems, particularly in organizations with a mix of legacy and modern applications. Legacy systems may not support modern SSO protocols, requiring custom solutions or additional middleware to bridge the gap. Additionally, organizations must carefully manage trust relationships between the identity provider and service providers to ensure secure and seamless communication.

The user experience is also a critical consideration when implementing SSO. While the primary goal is to simplify access, poorly designed SSO implementations can lead to confusion or frustration. For example, users may struggle with understanding when and how they are authenticated across different services, or they may encounter issues when their SSO session times out unexpectedly. To address these concerns, organizations must focus on clear communication, intuitive interfaces, and consistent user experiences across all applications.

Cloud computing and the rise of Software as a Service (SaaS) have further amplified the importance of SSO. As organizations increasingly rely on cloud-based applications for everything from email to project management, the need for a unified authentication solution has become critical. Many cloud service providers now offer built-in SSO capabilities, allowing organizations to integrate their existing identity management systems with cloud applications seamlessly. This integration not only simplifies access for users but also provides IT administrators with greater visibility and control over how and when applications are accessed.

Mobile devices present another frontier for SSO, as users expect the same seamless access on their smartphones and tablets as they do on their desktops. Mobile SSO solutions leverage device-based authentication methods, such as biometrics or device certificates, to provide secure and convenient access to applications. By combining these methods with traditional SSO protocols, organizations can extend seamless access to mobile environments while maintaining strong security.

The future of Single Sign-On is closely tied to the broader evolution of identity management and security technologies. Passwordless authentication, for example, represents a natural extension of SSO. By eliminating the need for passwords entirely and relying on biometrics, hardware tokens, or cryptographic keys, passwordless solutions can further simplify the authentication process while enhancing security. As these technologies mature, we can expect to see tighter integration with SSO systems, offering users a truly seamless and secure access experience.

Decentralized identity systems also hold promise for the future of SSO. In decentralized models, users have greater control over their identity data, often using blockchain technology to verify credentials without relying on a central authority. This approach aligns with the principles of SSO by enabling users to authenticate once and access multiple services, but it does so in a way that enhances privacy and reduces dependence on centralized identity providers.

Artificial intelligence and machine learning are increasingly being integrated into SSO systems to improve security and user experience. By analyzing user behavior and identifying anomalies, AI-driven systems can detect potential security threats in real-time and adjust authentication requirements accordingly. For example, if a user's behavior deviates from their typical patterns, the system might prompt for additional verification or temporarily restrict access. This adaptive approach enhances security while maintaining the seamless access that users expect from SSO.

Single Sign-On has become an indispensable tool in modern digital environments, offering a balance between security and convenience. By simplifying the authentication process and reducing the reliance on passwords, SSO not only enhances user experience but also strengthens organizational security. As technology continues to evolve, SSO will remain a cornerstone of identity management, adapting to new challenges and opportunities in the ever-changing digital landscape.

OAuth and OpenID Connect: Protocols that Power the Web

The modern web thrives on connectivity and seamless user experiences. As people increasingly rely on a variety of applications and services, the need for secure, efficient, and user-friendly authentication and authorization mechanisms has become paramount. Two protocols, OAuth and OpenID Connect, have emerged as foundational technologies that enable this secure interconnectivity. They are responsible for powering countless interactions behind the scenes, allowing users to log into websites with their social media accounts, granting apps access to personal data without sharing passwords, and maintaining the delicate balance between usability and security.

OAuth, short for Open Authorization, was introduced in 2010 as a protocol designed to provide secure, token-based authorization for third-party applications. Before OAuth, applications often had to rely on less secure methods, such as storing and using user credentials directly to access resources. This approach posed significant security risks, as it required users to trust third-party applications with their login information, increasing the likelihood of credential theft or misuse. OAuth revolutionized this process by introducing a way for users to grant limited access to their resources without sharing their passwords, using tokens as intermediaries.

At its core, OAuth operates through a system of roles and tokens. The primary roles include the resource owner (the user), the client (the application requesting access), the resource server (where the user's data is stored), and the authorization server (which issues access tokens). When a user wants to grant an application access to their data—say, allowing a photo-editing app to access their Google Drive photos—they are redirected to an authorization server managed by the resource provider, like Google. After the user consents to the requested permissions, the authorization server issues an access token to the client application. This token can then be used by the application to access the user's data, but only within the scope of the permissions granted.

One of the key strengths of OAuth is its flexibility in defining scopes and permissions. Scopes specify the level of access granted to the client application, allowing users to fine-tune what data they share. For example, a fitness tracking app might request access to a user's location data but not their contacts or email. This granular control empowers users to share only the information they are comfortable with, enhancing privacy and security.

Despite its widespread adoption and utility, OAuth is not an authentication protocol. It is primarily designed for authorization, meaning it determines what an application can do or access on behalf of a user, but it does not verify the identity of the user. This distinction led to the development of OpenID Connect, an identity layer built on top of OAuth 2.0. OpenID Connect extends OAuth's capabilities to include authentication, enabling applications to verify user identities while leveraging OAuth's robust authorization framework.

OpenID Connect introduces the concept of an ID token, which contains information about the authenticated user, such as their unique identifier, email address, and other profile details. When a user logs into an application using OpenID Connect—say, by clicking "Log in with Google" or "Sign in with Facebook"—the authorization server not only issues an access token for authorization but also an ID token for authentication. This ID token is digitally signed and can be verified by the client application to confirm the user's identity.

The synergy between OAuth and OpenID Connect has made them the de facto standards for securing user interactions on the web. Together, they provide a comprehensive solution for both authorization and authentication, enabling seamless and secure access across multiple applications and services. For example, a user might log into a social media platform using their Google account (authentication via OpenID Connect) and then allow a third-party game to post on their timeline (authorization via OAuth). This integration creates a smooth user experience while maintaining strong security protocols.

The impact of OAuth and OpenID Connect extends far beyond social media logins. These protocols are fundamental to the operation of modern APIs, which allow different software systems to communicate and share data. In an era where microservices architecture and cloud-based applications are the norm, secure API interactions are critical. OAuth provides a standardized way for services to authorize API requests, ensuring that only authenticated and authorized clients can access sensitive data. OpenID Connect complements this by adding user identity verification, enabling secure and personalized interactions within these systems.

The widespread adoption of OAuth and OpenID Connect has not only improved security but also simplified the development process for application developers. By relying on these standardized protocols, developers can integrate authentication and authorization features without reinventing the wheel. This consistency reduces the likelihood of security vulnerabilities, as developers can leverage well-tested libraries and services rather than implementing custom solutions prone to errors.

However, with great power comes great responsibility. The misuse or misconfiguration of OAuth and OpenID Connect can introduce security vulnerabilities, such as token leakage, insufficient token expiration, or improperly defined scopes. One common issue is the mistaken use of OAuth for authentication, known as the "confused deputy" problem. When developers incorrectly assume that OAuth's authorization tokens can be used to verify user identities, they inadvertently expose their applications to potential impersonation attacks. OpenID Connect addresses this issue by providing a clear, secure mechanism for authentication, but developers must be diligent in understanding the proper use of each protocol.

The security of OAuth and OpenID Connect also relies heavily on the secure management of tokens. Access tokens and ID tokens are the keys to accessing user data and verifying identities, so they must be protected from interception and misuse. Implementing secure token storage, using HTTPS for all communications, and applying best practices for token expiration and revocation are essential to maintaining the integrity of these protocols. Additionally, the introduction of Proof Key for Code Exchange (PKCE) has strengthened OAuth security, particularly for mobile and public clients, by mitigating the risk of authorization code interception.

As digital ecosystems continue to evolve, OAuth and OpenID Connect are adapting to meet new challenges and opportunities. The rise of decentralized identity systems, for example, is pushing the boundaries of traditional authentication and authorization models. In decentralized systems, users have greater control over their identity data, often using blockchain technology to verify credentials without relying on a central authority. While OAuth and OpenID Connect were designed for centralized systems, their principles are being extended and adapted to support decentralized identity frameworks, reflecting their flexibility and enduring relevance.

Another area of evolution is the growing emphasis on privacy and data protection. Regulations like the General Data Protection Regulation (GDPR) and the California Consumer Privacy Act (CCPA) have heightened awareness of data privacy issues, prompting organizations to implement more stringent controls over how user data is accessed and shared. OAuth's ability to define granular scopes and OpenID Connect's support for user consent mechanisms align well with these regulatory requirements, providing users with greater transparency and control over their personal information.

The future of OAuth and OpenID Connect is likely to be shaped by emerging technologies such as artificial intelligence, machine learning, and the Internet of Things (IoT). As more devices and services become interconnected, the need for secure, scalable authentication and authorization solutions will only grow. OAuth and OpenID Connect are well-positioned to meet these demands, offering a flexible framework that can be adapted to new contexts and use cases. Whether it's securing API interactions in a cloud-based application, enabling seamless logins across multiple platforms, or supporting decentralized identity initiatives, these protocols will continue to power the web's secure and seamless experiences.

Biometric Authentication: The Future of Identity

In a world where digital security is increasingly paramount, traditional authentication methods like passwords and PINs are proving insufficient to keep pace with evolving cyber threats. Users often struggle with managing numerous, complex passwords across various platforms, leading to weak security practices such as reusing credentials or choosing easily guessable combinations. Biometric authentication has emerged as a transformative solution, offering both enhanced security and greater convenience. By leveraging unique physiological and behavioral characteristics, biometric authentication represents the future of identity verification, promising a world where accessing sensitive information is both seamless and secure.

Biometric authentication operates on the principle that certain physical or behavioral traits are unique to individuals and can be used to reliably verify identity. These traits can include fingerprints, facial features, iris patterns, voice recognition, and even behavioral cues like typing rhythm or gait. Because these characteristics are intrinsic to each person, they are far more difficult to replicate or steal compared to traditional credentials. This inherent uniqueness makes biometrics an attractive option for strengthening security while simplifying the user experience.

The widespread adoption of biometric authentication can be traced back to the proliferation of smartphones equipped with fingerprint sensors and facial recognition capabilities. Apple's introduction of Touch ID in 2013, followed by Face ID in 2017, marked a turning point in mainstream acceptance of biometrics. These innovations demonstrated that biometric authentication could be both secure and user-friendly, allowing millions of people to unlock their devices, authorize payments, and access applications with a simple touch or glance. Other manufacturers quickly followed suit, embedding biometric sensors into a wide range of consumer electronics, from laptops to smart home devices.

One of the most compelling advantages of biometric authentication is its convenience. Unlike passwords, which must be remembered, typed, and periodically changed, biometrics require minimal effort from users. The process of scanning a fingerprint or recognizing a face is almost instantaneous, reducing friction in the authentication process. This ease of use is particularly valuable in mobile and wearable devices, where quick, secure access is essential for maintaining a smooth user experience.

However, the convenience of biometrics is matched by their potential to enhance security. Traditional authentication methods are susceptible to a variety of attacks, such as phishing, credential stuffing, and brute-force attempts. Biometrics, by contrast, are significantly more difficult to forge or steal. For example, while a password can be easily shared or leaked, replicating someone's fingerprint or facial features requires sophisticated technology and physical access to the individual. Furthermore, many biometric systems incorporate liveness detection features, designed to distinguish between real biometric traits and fake representations, such as photos or silicone fingerprints.

Despite these advantages, biometric authentication is not without its challenges and limitations. One of the primary concerns is the security of biometric data itself. Unlike passwords, which can be changed if compromised, biometric traits are immutable. If a biometric database is breached, the consequences can be severe and long-lasting, as affected individuals cannot simply replace their fingerprints or facial features. To mitigate this risk, biometric systems must employ robust encryption techniques and secure storage mechanisms, often using hardware-based solutions like Trusted Platform Modules (TPMs) or Secure Enclaves to protect sensitive data.

Another critical issue is privacy. The collection and storage of biometric data raise significant ethical and legal questions about how this information is used, who has access to it, and how long it is retained. Users must trust that organizations handling their biometric data will protect it responsibly and comply with relevant privacy regulations. In regions with stringent data protection laws, such as the European Union's General Data Protection Regulation (GDPR), companies are required to obtain explicit consent from users before collecting biometric data and must implement rigorous safeguards to prevent unauthorized access.

Moreover, biometric systems are not infallible and can be susceptible to false positives and false negatives. A false positive occurs when an unauthorized individual is mistakenly recognized as an authorized user, while a false negative happens when a legitimate user is denied access. These errors can result from various factors, such as poor image quality, environmental conditions, or changes in the user's appearance. For example, facial recognition systems may struggle in low-light environments or fail to recognize users who have significantly altered their appearance due to aging, facial hair, or cosmetic procedures. Ensuring the accuracy and reliability of biometric systems requires continuous refinement of algorithms and regular updates to accommodate a wide range of variables.

The implementation of biometric authentication also raises concerns about inclusivity and accessibility. Not all biometric systems work equally well for all individuals. For example, fingerprint scanners may have difficulty recognizing prints from individuals with certain skin conditions, manual laborers with worn fingerprints, or elderly users with less defined ridges. Similarly, facial recognition systems have been criticized for exhibiting biases, particularly in accurately identifying individuals from diverse demographic groups. Addressing these issues requires careful consideration in the design and testing of biometric technologies to ensure they are fair, inclusive, and accessible to all users.

Despite these challenges, the future of biometric authentication looks promising, driven by continuous advancements in technology and increasing demand for secure, user-friendly authentication methods. One of the key trends shaping this future is the integration of biometrics with multi-factor authentication (MFA). By combining biometric verification with other factors, such as a password or a security token, organizations can create layered security defenses that significantly reduce the risk of unauthorized access. This approach balances the convenience of biometrics with the added protection of multiple authentication factors.

Emerging biometric modalities are also expanding the possibilities for identity verification. Beyond traditional fingerprints and facial recognition, researchers are exploring new forms of biometric authentication, such as vein pattern recognition, heart rate signatures, and even brainwave analysis. These novel methods offer additional layers of uniqueness and security, further enhancing the potential of biometrics to serve as the cornerstone of digital identity. Behavioral biometrics, which analyze patterns in how users interact with devices—such as typing speed, mouse movements, or touchscreen gestures—are gaining traction as a way to provide continuous authentication without disrupting the user experience.

The rise of decentralized identity systems presents another exciting frontier for biometric authentication. In decentralized models, individuals have greater control over their identity data, often stored securely on personal devices rather than centralized servers. Biometrics can play a crucial role in these systems by providing a secure, user-centric method of verifying identity without relying on third-party intermediaries. This approach aligns with the growing emphasis on privacy and data sovereignty, allowing users to maintain ownership of their biometric data while still benefiting from the security and convenience of biometric authentication.

As biometric technology continues to evolve, its applications are expanding beyond personal devices and consumer services. Governments and organizations worldwide are leveraging biometrics for a wide range of purposes, from securing national borders and issuing digital IDs to streamlining access to healthcare, banking, and public services. In the financial sector, biometric authentication is being used to facilitate secure transactions and combat fraud, while in healthcare, it helps ensure that sensitive patient information is accessed only by authorized individuals.

The growing adoption of biometrics in public spaces also highlights the need for robust legal and ethical frameworks to guide their use. The deployment of facial recognition technology in surveillance, law enforcement, and public safety has sparked widespread debate over issues of privacy, consent, and potential misuse. Balancing the benefits of biometric authentication with the protection of individual rights will be crucial as societies navigate the complex intersection of technology, security, and civil liberties.

Biometric authentication represents a significant leap forward in the evolution of identity verification, offering a powerful combination of security, convenience, and innovation. While challenges remain in ensuring privacy, inclusivity, and ethical use, the ongoing development and refinement of biometric technologies are paving the way for a future where identity is not only secure but seamlessly integrated into our digital lives. As these technologies continue to mature, biometrics will play an increasingly central role in shaping the future of digital identity and the broader landscape of cybersecurity.

The Role of Identity Providers (IdPs)

In the ever-evolving digital landscape, managing identities securely and efficiently has become a cornerstone of modern technology infrastructure. At the heart of this identity ecosystem are Identity Providers (IdPs), entities that play a crucial role in authenticating users and facilitating secure access to resources across various platforms and services. As organizations and individuals navigate a world increasingly reliant on interconnected systems, understanding the function and importance of Identity Providers is essential to grasp how secure, seamless digital interactions are made possible.

An Identity Provider is a trusted entity responsible for verifying the identity of users and issuing authentication tokens that enable access to multiple services. Instead of requiring users to create separate credentials for every application they use, IdPs allow for centralized authentication. This means that once a user's identity is confirmed by the IdP, they can seamlessly access different services without needing to log in repeatedly. This concept is foundational to Single Sign-On (SSO) systems, which have become a standard feature in both enterprise and consumer applications, significantly enhancing user convenience while maintaining robust security protocols.

The primary function of an Identity Provider is authentication—the process of confirming that a user is who they claim to be. When a user attempts to log into an application, the application redirects them to the IdP, which requests the necessary credentials. These credentials can take various forms, from traditional usernames and passwords to more advanced methods like biometric data or multi-factor authentication (MFA). Once the IdP successfully authenticates the user, it generates an authentication token, typically following protocols like SAML (Security Assertion Markup Language), OAuth, or OpenID Connect. This token is then sent back to the application, granting the user access without the need for direct credential exchange between the user and the application.

Beyond authentication, Identity Providers also play a significant role in authorization, determining what resources or services a user is permitted to access. While the primary responsibility for authorization often lies with the service provider, IdPs contribute by embedding specific claims or attributes within the authentication tokens they issue. These claims might include information about the user's role, group membership, or specific permissions, enabling service providers to make informed decisions about what level of access to grant. This integration of authentication and authorization simplifies access management, particularly in large organizations where users need to interact with a wide range of applications and resources.

One of the key benefits of using an Identity Provider is the enhanced security it offers. By centralizing authentication, IdPs reduce the risks associated with managing multiple sets of credentials across various platforms. This centralized approach allows organizations to enforce consistent security policies, such as password complexity requirements, multi-factor authentication, and account lockout mechanisms. It also simplifies the process of monitoring and auditing authentication activities, enabling quicker detection of suspicious behavior or potential security breaches.

Identity Providers also play a vital role in reducing the administrative burden associated with identity and access management. For organizations, managing user accounts individually across numerous applications can be time-consuming and prone to errors. IdPs streamline this process by providing a single point of control for user authentication and access. When a new employee joins an organization, IT administrators can quickly provision access to all necessary applications through the IdP. Conversely, when an employee leaves, disabling their account at the IdP level effectively revokes their access to all connected services, mitigating the risk of orphaned accounts that could be exploited by malicious actors.

The flexibility of Identity Providers extends to their ability to support federated identity management, a system that allows users to access resources across different organizations using a single set of credentials. This capability is particularly valuable in scenarios where businesses need to collaborate with external partners, contractors, or clients. By establishing trust relationships between different IdPs, federated identity systems enable seamless, secure access to shared resources without the need for duplicate accounts or credentials. For example, an employee from one company might be able to access a partner organization's internal systems using their existing corporate credentials, streamlining collaboration while maintaining strong security controls.

The concept of federated identity is often implemented through protocols like SAML and OpenID Connect, which standardize the way authentication and authorization data are exchanged between Identity Providers and service providers. These protocols ensure interoperability between different systems and platforms, making it easier for organizations to integrate their IdPs with third-party applications and services. This interoperability is a critical feature in today's diverse IT environments, where organizations rely on a mix of on-premises systems, cloud-based applications, and mobile platforms.

Cloud computing has further amplified the importance of Identity Providers. As organizations increasingly adopt cloud services, managing identities across multiple cloud platforms has become a complex challenge. Cloud-based IdPs, such as Microsoft Azure Active Directory, Okta, and Google Identity, offer scalable, flexible solutions for managing user identities in hybrid environments that span on-premises and cloud infrastructure. These cloud IdPs provide robust authentication and authorization services, along with features like single sign-on, multi-factor authentication, and identity governance, enabling organizations to maintain consistent security policies and user experiences across diverse environments.

The rise of Identity as a Service (IDaaS) platforms reflects the growing demand for outsourced identity management solutions. IDaaS providers offer comprehensive identity and access management services delivered through the cloud, allowing organizations to offload the complexities of managing IdPs to specialized vendors. These services include not only authentication and authorization but also user provisioning, directory services, and compliance reporting. By leveraging IDaaS, organizations can focus on their core business activities while ensuring that their identity management needs are handled by experts with the latest security technologies and best practices.

Despite the many advantages of Identity Providers, there are challenges and risks associated with their use. One of the primary concerns is the potential for a single point of failure. Because IdPs serve as the central authority for authentication, a compromise or outage at the IdP level can disrupt access to all connected services. To mitigate this risk, organizations must implement robust security measures, such as redundant IdP configurations, strong encryption, and continuous monitoring for anomalies. Additionally, incorporating multi-factor authentication adds an extra layer of security, reducing the likelihood of unauthorized access even if an IdP is targeted.

Another critical consideration is privacy. Identity Providers handle sensitive personal information, including credentials, user attributes, and access logs. Ensuring that this data is protected and used responsibly is essential for maintaining user trust and complying with data protection regulations like the General Data Protection Regulation (GDPR) and the California Consumer Privacy Act (CCPA). Organizations must establish clear policies for data collection, storage, and sharing, and ensure that users are informed about how their information is being used. Transparency and user consent are key components of responsible identity management practices.

As technology continues to evolve, the role of Identity Providers is expanding to address new challenges and opportunities. The growing adoption of decentralized identity systems represents a significant shift in how identities are managed and verified. In decentralized models, individuals have greater control over their identity data, often stored on personal devices or distributed across blockchain networks. While traditional IdPs rely on centralized authority, decentralized identity systems use cryptographic techniques to enable secure, user-controlled authentication. This approach aligns with the principles of privacy and data sovereignty, empowering users to manage their identities without relying on third-party intermediaries.

Artificial intelligence and machine learning are also being integrated into Identity Provider systems to enhance security and user experience. By analyzing patterns of user behavior and detecting anomalies in real time, AI-driven IdPs can identify potential security threats and respond proactively. For example, if a user's login attempt deviates from their typical behavior—such as logging in from an unusual location or device—the IdP can trigger additional authentication requirements or temporarily restrict access. This adaptive approach enhances security while maintaining a smooth user experience.

Identity Providers are indispensable components of the modern digital ecosystem, enabling secure, seamless access to applications and services across diverse environments. By centralizing authentication, simplifying access management, and supporting federated identity, IdPs play a critical role in enhancing security, improving user experience, and reducing administrative overhead. As technology and security needs continue to evolve, Identity Providers will remain at the forefront of identity and access management, adapting to new challenges and driving innovation in how digital identities are managed and protected.

Federated Identity: Crossing Organizational Boundaries

In an increasingly interconnected digital world, the need for secure and seamless access to systems across organizational boundaries has become more important than ever. Businesses, educational institutions, government agencies, and even individuals rely on multiple systems that must interact efficiently while maintaining strict security protocols. This necessity has led to the rise of federated identity, a framework that allows users to access resources across different organizations using a single set of credentials. By enabling cross-domain authentication and fostering trust relationships between entities, federated identity simplifies access management, enhances security, and improves user experience.

Federated identity is built on the principle of trust between organizations. In a federated system, multiple organizations—each with their own identity management systems—agree to recognize and accept each other's authentication processes. This means that a user authenticated by one organization, known as the identity provider (IdP), can access resources in another organization, referred to as the service provider (SP), without needing to create separate credentials. This trust relationship is facilitated through standardized protocols like Security Assertion Markup Language (SAML), OpenID Connect, and OAuth, which allow identity information to be securely shared between entities.

The primary advantage of federated identity is the ability to streamline access across multiple systems and domains. In traditional, siloed identity management models, users are required to maintain separate credentials for each application or organization they interact with. This not only leads to password fatigue but also increases security risks due to weak, reused, or forgotten passwords. Federated identity eliminates the need for multiple credentials, allowing users to authenticate once and gain access to a range of resources across different organizations. This approach enhances the user experience, reduces administrative overhead, and strengthens security by minimizing the attack surface associated with credential management.

Federated identity is particularly valuable in environments where collaboration between organizations is essential. For example, in higher education, federated identity allows students, faculty, and researchers to access resources across multiple institutions using their home institution credentials. Initiatives like the InCommon Federation in the United States and eduGAIN in Europe enable secure, seamless access to shared academic resources, research tools, and library databases, fostering greater collaboration and knowledge sharing within the academic community.

In the business world, federated identity facilitates partnerships, supply chain interactions, and customer relationships by enabling secure access to shared systems and applications. Companies that work closely with vendors, contractors, or partner organizations can use federated identity to provide external users with access to internal resources without compromising security or requiring complex account management processes. For example, a manufacturer might grant a supplier access to its inventory management system through federated authentication, ensuring that the supplier can update stock levels and track shipments without needing separate login credentials.

Government agencies also benefit from federated identity frameworks, particularly in scenarios where citizens or employees need to access services across different departments or jurisdictions. National and regional federations can streamline access to public services, enabling users to authenticate once and interact with multiple government platforms, from tax filing systems to healthcare portals. This unified approach not only improves the efficiency of public service delivery but also enhances security by centralizing authentication and reducing the risk of unauthorized access.

The technical foundation of federated identity relies on standardized protocols that ensure secure, interoperable communication between identity providers and service providers. SAML is one of the most widely used protocols in federated identity systems, particularly in enterprise and academic environments. SAML enables the exchange of authentication and authorization data between organizations using XML-based assertions. When a user attempts to access a service provider's application, the service provider redirects the user to their home identity provider for authentication. Once authenticated, the identity provider issues a SAML assertion containing information about the user's identity and permissions, which the service provider uses to grant access.

OpenID Connect, built on top of the OAuth 2.0 framework, is another popular protocol for federated identity, particularly in web and mobile applications. OpenID Connect extends OAuth's authorization capabilities to include authentication, allowing users to log into third-party applications using their existing credentials from trusted identity providers like Google, Microsoft, or Facebook. This protocol simplifies the integration of federated identity in consumer-facing applications, enabling seamless login experiences across different platforms and services.

The adoption of federated identity brings numerous security benefits, but it also introduces new challenges that organizations must address. One of the primary security advantages is the reduction of password-related vulnerabilities. By minimizing the number of credentials users need to manage, federated identity reduces the likelihood of weak or reused passwords, as well as the risk of phishing attacks targeting credential theft. Additionally, centralized authentication through a trusted identity provider allows organizations to enforce consistent security policies, such as multi-factor authentication, across all connected services.

However, the reliance on trust relationships between organizations introduces potential risks. If an identity provider is compromised, the attacker could gain access to all service providers that trust that identity provider, potentially leading to widespread data breaches or unauthorized access. To mitigate this risk, organizations must establish strict criteria for selecting trusted identity providers and implement robust monitoring and auditing processes to detect and respond to suspicious activity. Regular reviews of trust relationships and adherence to best practices in identity federation are essential to maintaining the integrity of the system.

Privacy is another critical consideration in federated identity systems. The exchange of identity information between organizations raises questions about data protection, user consent, and transparency. Organizations must ensure that personal data is handled responsibly and in compliance with relevant privacy regulations, such as the General Data Protection Regulation (GDPR) and the California Consumer Privacy Act (CCPA). This includes obtaining explicit user consent before sharing identity information, limiting the scope of data exchanged to what is necessary for authentication, and providing users with clear information about how their data is being used.

The success of federated identity systems also depends on interoperability and standardization. Organizations participating in a federation must adhere to common protocols and standards to ensure seamless communication and compatibility between different identity and service providers. Initiatives like the Kantara Initiative and the OpenID Foundation play a vital role in developing and promoting these standards, fostering a collaborative approach to identity management that benefits all participants.

As technology continues to evolve, federated identity is adapting to meet new challenges and opportunities. The rise of cloud computing and the increasing reliance on SaaS applications have amplified the need for federated identity solutions that can span both on-premises and cloud environments. Cloud-based identity providers, such as Microsoft Azure Active Directory and Okta, offer federated identity services that integrate seamlessly with a wide range of cloud applications, enabling organizations to manage user identities consistently across diverse platforms.

Decentralized identity systems represent an emerging frontier in federated identity, shifting the focus from centralized trust relationships to user-controlled identity management. In decentralized models, users store their identity credentials securely on personal devices or distributed ledger technologies, such as blockchain. These systems allow users to authenticate across multiple organizations without relying on a central identity provider, enhancing privacy and data sovereignty. While decentralized identity is still in its early stages, it holds the potential to transform the way federated identity systems operate, offering greater flexibility and user empowerment.

Artificial intelligence and machine learning are also being integrated into federated identity systems to enhance security and user experience. By analyzing patterns of user behavior and detecting anomalies in real-time, AI-driven systems can identify potential security threats and adjust authentication requirements accordingly. For example, if a user's login attempt deviates from their typical behavior, such as accessing resources from an unusual location or device, the system can trigger additional verification steps or flag the activity for further investigation.

Federated identity has become an essential component of modern identity and access management, enabling secure, seamless access to resources across organizational boundaries. By fostering trust relationships between entities, simplifying credential management, and enhancing security, federated identity supports collaboration and innovation in a wide range of environments, from academia and business to government and healthcare. As technology continues to evolve, federated identity will remain at the forefront of efforts to create a more connected, secure, and user-friendly digital ecosystem.

Decentralized Identity: Blockchain and Beyond

In the rapidly evolving digital world, managing identity securely and efficiently has become one of the most pressing challenges. Traditional identity systems rely heavily on centralized authorities like governments, corporations, or third-party providers to issue, manage, and verify identities. While these centralized systems offer convenience, they come with significant risks, including data breaches, privacy concerns, and lack of user control over personal information. As the demand for more secure, private, and user-centric identity solutions grows, decentralized identity has emerged as a promising alternative. Powered by blockchain technology and innovative cryptographic techniques, decentralized identity shifts control from centralized authorities to individuals, paving the way for a more secure and transparent digital future.

Decentralized identity is based on the concept of self-sovereign identity (SSI), which gives individuals full ownership and control over their personal data. Unlike traditional systems, where identity information is stored and managed by centralized databases, decentralized identity solutions allow users to store their credentials in digital wallets on their personal devices. These credentials can be selectively shared with third parties when needed, without exposing unnecessary information. For example, instead of presenting a full driver's license to prove one's age at a bar, a person could share only the fact that they are over the legal drinking age, without revealing their name, address, or birthdate. This selective disclosure not only enhances privacy but also reduces the risk of identity theft and data misuse.

Blockchain technology plays a crucial role in enabling decentralized identity systems. A blockchain is a distributed ledger that records transactions in a secure, immutable, and transparent manner. In the context of decentralized identity, blockchain is used to create a tamper-proof record of identity credentials and verifications. While the actual personal data is not stored on the blockchain, the ledger contains cryptographic proofs that verify the authenticity of credentials without revealing sensitive information. This approach ensures that identity data remains secure and verifiable, while users retain control over their own information.

One of the key components of decentralized identity systems is the use of decentralized identifiers (DIDs). DIDs are unique, cryptographically verifiable identifiers that are not tied to any central authority. They are created and managed by the individual, giving them full control over their digital identity. DIDs are stored on the blockchain, providing a public, tamper-resistant reference that can be used to verify credentials. When a user presents a credential to a service provider, the provider can check the associated DID on the blockchain to confirm its validity, without needing to contact a central issuing authority.

Verifiable credentials are another essential element of decentralized identity. These are digital certificates that contain claims about an individual, such as their name, qualifications, or membership in an organization. Verifiable credentials are issued by trusted entities, such as universities, employers, or government agencies, and are cryptographically signed to ensure their authenticity. The individual receives these credentials and stores them in their digital wallet, from where they can share them as needed. When a credential is presented, the verifier can use the cryptographic signature and the corresponding DID on the blockchain to confirm that the credential is genuine and has not been altered.

The advantages of decentralized identity are numerous and far-reaching. One of the most significant benefits is enhanced privacy. Traditional identity systems often require individuals to share excessive amounts of personal information, leading to unnecessary exposure and increased risk of data breaches. Decentralized identity allows for selective disclosure, enabling users to share only the information necessary for a specific transaction. This minimizes the amount of personal data in circulation and reduces the likelihood of unauthorized access or misuse.

Security is another major advantage of decentralized identity. Centralized databases are prime targets for hackers, as they contain vast amounts of sensitive information in a single location. Data breaches at major corporations and institutions have exposed the personal information of millions of people, leading to identity theft, financial fraud, and other malicious activities. By distributing identity data across individual devices and using blockchain for verification, decentralized identity eliminates the single point of failure inherent in centralized systems. Even if a user's device is compromised, the attacker would not gain access to a centralized repository of information.

Decentralized identity also offers greater user autonomy and control. In traditional systems, individuals have little say over how their data is collected, stored, and used. Service providers often retain control over user information, leading to issues of data ownership and consent. With decentralized identity, users are in charge of their own data, deciding when, how, and with whom to share their credentials. This shift in control empowers individuals, promotes transparency, and fosters trust in digital interactions.

The potential applications of decentralized identity are vast and varied, spanning multiple industries and sectors. In finance, decentralized identity can streamline the process of verifying customer identities for Know Your Customer (KYC) and Anti-Money Laundering (AML) compliance. Financial institutions can rely on verifiable credentials issued by trusted entities, reducing the need for repetitive and time-consuming identity checks. This not only improves efficiency but also enhances security and reduces costs.

In healthcare, decentralized identity can facilitate secure and private access to medical records. Patients can store their health data in digital wallets and share it with healthcare providers as needed, ensuring that their information remains confidential and under their control. This approach can improve patient care, enhance data security, and reduce administrative burdens in healthcare systems.

Education is another sector poised to benefit from decentralized identity. Academic institutions can issue verifiable credentials for diplomas, certifications, and transcripts, which students can store and share with potential employers or other educational institutions. This simplifies the verification process, reduces the risk of credential fraud, and provides a secure, permanent record of academic achievements.

Government services can also leverage decentralized identity to improve public service delivery and enhance citizen trust. By enabling secure, user-controlled access to digital services, governments can streamline processes such as voting, tax filing, and social security benefits. Decentralized identity can also support digital inclusion by providing secure identity solutions to individuals who lack traditional forms of identification, such as refugees or those living in remote areas.

Despite its many advantages, decentralized identity faces several challenges and barriers to widespread adoption. One of the primary challenges is interoperability. For decentralized identity systems to be effective, they must be compatible with existing identity infrastructure and standards. Ensuring seamless integration with current systems and achieving broad consensus on standards and protocols is essential for the success of decentralized identity initiatives.

Another challenge is user adoption and education. Decentralized identity represents a significant shift from traditional identity management models, and many users may be unfamiliar with the concepts and technologies involved. Educating individuals and organizations about the benefits and practicalities of decentralized identity is crucial to driving adoption. Additionally, ensuring that decentralized identity solutions are user-friendly and accessible to people of all technical skill levels is essential to achieving widespread use.

Privacy and regulatory compliance are also critical considerations in the development and deployment of decentralized identity systems. While decentralized identity offers enhanced privacy features, it must also comply with data protection regulations such as the General Data Protection Regulation (GDPR) and the California Consumer Privacy Act (CCPA). Ensuring that decentralized identity solutions adhere to legal requirements while maintaining user privacy and control is a complex but necessary task.

The future of decentralized identity is bright, with ongoing advancements in blockchain technology, cryptographic techniques, and digital identity standards paving the way for broader adoption. As more organizations, governments, and individuals recognize the benefits of decentralized identity, we can expect to see an increasing number of innovative applications and use cases. From finance and healthcare to education and government services, decentralized identity has the potential to transform the way we manage and protect our digital identities, creating a more secure, private, and user-centric digital world.

Role-Based Access Control (RBAC) Explained

In the digital age, where organizations manage vast amounts of sensitive data and operate complex systems, controlling who has access to what information is crucial. Without a structured approach to managing permissions, organizations risk exposing themselves to data breaches, unauthorized actions, and operational inefficiencies. Role-Based Access Control (RBAC) has emerged as one of the most effective frameworks for managing permissions in a scalable, secure, and efficient manner. By assigning access rights based on defined roles within an organization, RBAC simplifies the process of managing permissions, enhances security, and ensures that users have access only to the resources necessary for their job functions.

RBAC is a policy-neutral access control mechanism that restricts system access to authorized users based on their role within an organization. A role in RBAC represents a collection of permissions that correspond to the responsibilities associated with a particular job function. Instead of assigning permissions to individual users directly, permissions are assigned to roles, and users are then assigned to those roles. This abstraction layer simplifies permission management, particularly in large organizations with many users and complex access requirements.

The concept of RBAC is rooted in the principle of least privilege, which states that users should be granted the minimum level of access necessary to perform their job duties. By limiting access to only what is required, organizations reduce the risk of accidental or intentional misuse of data and resources. For example, a marketing employee may need access to customer engagement data but should not have permissions to modify financial records. Conversely, an accountant might require access to financial systems but not to marketing analytics. RBAC ensures that each user's access is aligned with their role, reducing the likelihood of unauthorized actions.

One of the primary benefits of RBAC is its ability to simplify the management of user permissions. In traditional access control models, administrators must assign permissions to each user individually, which can become unmanageable as the number of users and resources grows. This approach is not only time-consuming but also prone to errors, such as granting excessive permissions or failing to revoke access when a user's role changes. RBAC addresses these challenges by centralizing permission management at the role level. When a user joins the organization, they are assigned to a role based on their job function, automatically granting them the appropriate permissions. If their responsibilities change, administrators can simply reassign the user to a different role, ensuring their access rights are always up to date.

RBAC is particularly valuable in dynamic environments where users frequently change roles, join new projects, or transition between departments. In such settings, managing permissions on an individual basis can quickly become overwhelming. RBAC provides a flexible and scalable solution, allowing organizations to define roles that reflect their internal·structure and business processes. Roles can be as broad or granular as needed, depending on the organization's requirements. For example, a small company might have roles like "Employee," "Manager," and "Administrator," while a larger organization might define more specific roles such as "HR Specialist," "IT Support Technician," or "Sales Representative."

The implementation of RBAC typically involves several key components: roles, permissions, users, and role hierarchies. Roles are defined based on job functions, and each role is associated with a set of permissions that specify what actions can be performed and on which resources. Users are assigned to roles, inheriting the permissions associated with those roles. Role hierarchies allow for the creation of more complex access control structures, where roles can inherit permissions from other roles. For example, a "Manager" role might inherit all the permissions of the "Employee" role, in addition to having extra permissions for approving requests or accessing higher-level reports.

RBAC is widely used across various industries and applications, from corporate IT systems and cloud services to healthcare, finance, and government operations. In healthcare, RBAC helps protect sensitive patient data by ensuring that only authorized personnel, such as doctors and nurses, can access medical records, while administrative staff have restricted access based on their roles. In finance, RBAC ensures that traders, accountants, and auditors have appropriate access to financial systems without compromising sensitive information. In government, RBAC is used to manage access to classified information, ensuring that only individuals with the appropriate clearance can view or modify sensitive data.

While RBAC offers numerous advantages, it is not without its challenges. One of the primary challenges is role design and management. Defining roles that accurately reflect an organization's structure and access requirements can be complex, particularly in large or rapidly changing environments. Poorly designed roles can lead to over-permissioning, where users have more access than necessary, or under-permissioning, where users are unable to perform their job duties effectively. To address this, organizations must regularly review and update their role definitions to ensure they remain aligned with current business needs and security policies.

Another challenge is the potential for role explosion, a situation where the number of roles within an organization becomes unmanageable. This can occur when roles are defined too narrowly, leading to a proliferation of highly specific roles that are difficult to maintain. To prevent role explosion, organizations should strive for a balance between granularity and simplicity, grouping similar job functions under broader roles where appropriate. Role hierarchies and the use of role templates can also help manage complexity by enabling the reuse and inheritance of permissions across different roles.

RBAC is often compared to other access control models, such as Discretionary Access Control (DAC) and Attribute-Based Access Control (ABAC). In DAC, resource owners have the discretion to grant or revoke access to their resources, which can lead to inconsistent and decentralized permission management. ABAC, on the other hand, uses attributes—such as user characteristics, resource types, and environmental conditions—to determine access rights dynamically. While ABAC offers greater flexibility and fine-grained control, it can also be more complex to implement and manage. RBAC strikes a balance between simplicity and control, making it an attractive choice for many organizations seeking a scalable and manageable access control solution.

The integration of RBAC with modern technologies and identity management systems further enhances its capabilities. Many organizations implement RBAC in conjunction with Identity and Access Management (IAM) solutions, which provide centralized control over user identities and access rights. IAM systems often include features such as automated role assignment, audit logging, and compliance reporting, making it easier to enforce RBAC policies and demonstrate regulatory compliance. Cloud service providers, such as Amazon Web Services (AWS), Microsoft Azure, and Google Cloud, also offer RBAC features, allowing organizations to manage access to cloud resources based on predefined roles.

The future of RBAC is likely to be shaped by emerging trends in technology and security. The rise of hybrid and multi-cloud environments, the increasing use of microservices and APIs, and the growing importance of data privacy and regulatory compliance are driving the need for more sophisticated access control models. While RBAC will continue to play a central role in managing permissions, it is increasingly being combined with other models, such as ABAC and policy-based access control (PBAC), to provide more dynamic and context-aware access management. These hybrid approaches leverage the strengths of RBAC's role-based structure while incorporating additional factors, such as user attributes and environmental conditions, to refine access decisions.

Artificial intelligence and machine learning are also being explored as tools to enhance RBAC systems. By analyzing user behavior and access patterns, AI-driven systems can identify anomalies, suggest role adjustments, and detect potential security threats in real-time. This proactive approach to access management not only improves security but also ensures that roles and permissions remain aligned with actual usage and organizational needs.

Role-Based Access Control has proven to be a reliable and effective method for managing access in a wide range of environments. By aligning permissions with job functions, RBAC simplifies the administration of user access, enhances security through the principle of least privilege, and provides a scalable framework that can adapt to organizational growth and change. As technology continues to evolve, RBAC will remain a fundamental component of access management, evolving alongside other models and technologies to meet the demands of an increasingly complex and interconnected digital world.

Attribute-Based Access Control (ABAC): A Flexible Approach

As organizations navigate the challenges of securing digital environments, access control has become a critical component of cybersecurity strategies. While traditional models like Role-Based Access Control (RBAC) have served well in many contexts, they can sometimes be too rigid to accommodate the dynamic and complex nature of modern IT ecosystems. This is where Attribute-Based Access Control (ABAC) steps in, offering a more flexible and fine-grained approach to managing permissions. By using a combination of attributes to determine access rights, ABAC allows organizations to create highly customizable and context-aware access policies that adapt to evolving business needs and security requirements.

At its core, ABAC is a policy-based access control model that uses attributes to govern access decisions. Attributes are descriptive characteristics associated with users, resources, actions, and the environment. These can include user attributes like job title, department, security clearance, or age; resource attributes such as data classification, file type, or ownership; action attributes like read, write, or delete permissions; and environmental attributes, including time of day, location, or device type. By evaluating these attributes against predefined policies, ABAC determines whether a user should be granted or denied access to a particular resource.

One of the defining features of ABAC is its flexibility. Unlike RBAC, which relies on predefined roles and static permission assignments, ABAC allows for dynamic access control based on a wide range of contextual factors. This means that access decisions can be tailored to specific situations, enabling more granular and precise control over who can access what, when, and under what conditions. For example, an employee might have access to sensitive financial data during business hours from a secure office location but be restricted from accessing the same data remotely or outside of working hours. This level of specificity is difficult to achieve with role-based models alone.

The flexibility of ABAC makes it particularly well-suited for organizations with complex and diverse access control requirements. In industries such as healthcare, finance, and government, where sensitive data must be protected under strict regulatory frameworks, ABAC provides the ability to enforce nuanced access policies that align with compliance requirements. For instance, a hospital might use ABAC to ensure that only authorized medical staff can access patient records, and even then, only those records relevant to their current cases. Similarly, a financial institution might use ABAC to restrict access to confidential data based on an employee's role, location, and the sensitivity of the data being accessed.

The implementation of ABAC typically involves four key components: attributes, policies, policy decision points (PDPs), and policy enforcement points (PEPs). Attributes are collected and managed in a central repository or derived from existing identity and resource management systems. Policies are defined using a policy language, such as eXtensible Access Control Markup Language (XACML), which specifies the rules and conditions under which access should be granted or denied. The PDP evaluates access requests against these policies, using the relevant attributes to make decisions. The PEP enforces these decisions by granting or denying access to the requested resources.

One of the primary advantages of ABAC is its scalability. In large organizations with thousands of users and resources, managing access through individual permissions or even roles can become unmanageable. ABAC addresses this challenge by abstracting access control decisions from specific users and roles, focusing instead on attributes and policies that can apply universally. This abstraction allows organizations to define a relatively small set of policies that can cover a wide range of scenarios, reducing administrative overhead and simplifying access management.

ABAC also enhances security by supporting the principle of least privilege, which ensures that users have only the minimum access necessary to perform their duties. By evaluating access requests in real-time based on current attributes and context, ABAC minimizes the risk of over-permissioning and reduces the attack surface for potential security breaches. For example, if an employee's job responsibilities change, their access rights automatically adjust based on their updated attributes, without requiring manual intervention from administrators.

Despite its many benefits, ABAC is not without challenges. One of the most significant challenges is the complexity of policy management. Defining and maintaining comprehensive, consistent, and conflict-free policies can be difficult, particularly in organizations with diverse and dynamic access control requirements. Poorly designed policies can lead to unintended access denials or permissions, potentially disrupting business operations or exposing sensitive data to unauthorized users. To mitigate these risks, organizations must invest in robust policy management tools and processes, including regular policy reviews, testing, and auditing.

Another challenge is the integration of ABAC with existing systems and infrastructure. Many organizations already have established identity management and access control frameworks, such as RBAC or Discretionary Access Control (DAC). Integrating ABAC into these environments requires careful planning to ensure compatibility and avoid disruptions. This may involve mapping existing roles and permissions to attributes, updating legacy systems to support attribute-based policies, and training administrators and users on the new access control model.

Performance is another consideration in ABAC implementations. Because ABAC evaluates access requests dynamically based on multiple attributes and policies, it can introduce latency in high-traffic environments. Ensuring that the PDP and PEP components are optimized for performance is essential to maintaining a seamless user experience. This might involve caching frequently used attributes, distributing policy evaluation across multiple servers, or employing efficient policy decision algorithms.

Despite these challenges, the adoption of ABAC is growing as organizations recognize its potential to address the complexities of modern access control. The rise of cloud computing, mobile workforces, and interconnected systems has created environments where traditional access control models struggle to keep pace. ABAC's ability to provide fine-grained, context-aware access control makes it an ideal solution for these dynamic and distributed environments.

In cloud environments, ABAC enables organizations to manage access across multiple cloud services and platforms using a unified set of policies and attributes. Cloud service providers, such as Amazon Web Services (AWS), Microsoft Azure, and Google Cloud, offer ABAC capabilities that allow organizations to define access control policies based on attributes like resource tags, user properties, and environmental conditions. This approach simplifies the management of cloud resources, enhances security, and supports compliance with regulatory requirements.

ABAC also plays a critical role in supporting data privacy and protection initiatives. As organizations face increasing pressure to safeguard personal data and comply with privacy regulations like the General Data Protection Regulation (GDPR) and the California Consumer Privacy Act (CCPA), ABAC provides a powerful tool for enforcing data access policies. By using attributes to control who can access specific data and under what conditions, organizations can ensure that personal information is only accessible to authorized users and for legitimate purposes.

The future of ABAC is closely tied to advancements in artificial intelligence (AI) and machine learning (ML). By integrating AI and ML capabilities into ABAC systems, organizations can enhance policy creation, management, and enforcement. For example, machine learning algorithms can analyze user behavior and access patterns to identify anomalies, recommend policy adjustments, and detect potential security threats. AI-driven ABAC systems can also automate the process of attribute assignment and policy refinement, reducing administrative effort and improving the accuracy of access control decisions.

Another emerging trend is the combination of ABAC with other access control models, such as RBAC and Policy-Based Access Control (PBAC), to create hybrid solutions that leverage the strengths of each approach. While RBAC provides a straightforward and easy-to-manage framework for defining roles and permissions, ABAC adds the flexibility to refine access decisions based on dynamic attributes and contextual factors. By combining these models, organizations can achieve a balance between simplicity and flexibility, ensuring that their access control systems are both effective and adaptable.

Attribute-Based Access Control represents a significant evolution in the way organizations manage access to digital resources. By leveraging a wide range of attributes and policies, ABAC offers a flexible, scalable, and secure approach to access control that can adapt to the complexities of modern IT environments. As organizations continue to embrace digital transformation, cloud computing, and data privacy initiatives, ABAC will play an increasingly important role in ensuring that access to sensitive information is managed effectively and securely. Through careful implementation, robust policy management, and ongoing integration with emerging technologies, ABAC provides a foundation for the next generation of access control solutions.

Policy-Based Access Control (PBAC): Rules Over Roles

As digital ecosystems become increasingly complex and interconnected, the need for sophisticated access control mechanisms has never been more critical. Traditional models like Role-Based Access Control (RBAC) and Attribute-Based Access Control (ABAC) have served organizations well in managing permissions and safeguarding sensitive data. However, the dynamic nature of modern enterprises, cloud computing environments, and regulatory landscapes calls for even more flexible and granular control over access rights. Policy-Based Access Control (PBAC) emerges as a powerful solution to meet these evolving demands, emphasizing rules and policies over static roles to govern access decisions.

Policy-Based Access Control is an advanced access management model that relies on pre-defined policies to determine who can access specific resources under particular conditions. Unlike RBAC, which assigns permissions based on a user's role within an organization, PBAC evaluates access requests against a set of dynamic, context-aware rules. These policies can incorporate a variety of factors, including user attributes, resource characteristics, environmental conditions, and even real-time contextual information such as user behavior or location. By focusing on policies rather than static roles, PBAC provides organizations with a highly flexible and adaptable framework for managing access control.

The core strength of PBAC lies in its ability to make dynamic, context-sensitive access decisions. In traditional role-based systems, access rights are often broad and static, making it difficult to account for the nuances of real-world scenarios. For example, an employee with a managerial role might have unrestricted access to certain financial data, regardless of whether they need it at a given moment. PBAC, on the other hand, can evaluate whether the employee's current context—such as their location, the time of day, or the sensitivity of the data—justifies granting access. This approach ensures that permissions are granted only when appropriate, reducing the risk of unauthorized access and data breaches.

Policies in PBAC are typically defined using high-level, human-readable languages that allow administrators to express complex access rules clearly and concisely. These policies specify the conditions under which access should be granted or denied, often using logical expressions and conditional statements. For example, a policy might state, "Allow access to confidential financial reports if the user is part of the finance department, accessing from a secure network, and during business hours." By encapsulating access rules in policies, PBAC separates the decision-making logic from the underlying system architecture, making it easier to manage, update, and audit access controls.

One of the key components of PBAC is the policy decision point (PDP), which evaluates access requests against the defined policies and determines whether to grant or deny access. When a user attempts to access a resource, the request is sent to the PDP, which considers all relevant factors and applies the appropriate policies to make a decision. The policy enforcement point (PEP) then enforces this decision by granting or denying access to the requested resource. This separation of decision-making and enforcement allows for greater flexibility and scalability, as policies can be updated or modified without altering the underlying system infrastructure.

PBAC offers several advantages over traditional access control models. One of the most significant benefits is its ability to provide fine-grained, context-aware access control. By considering a wide range of factors in access decisions, PBAC can accommodate complex and dynamic access requirements that static role-based models cannot. This is particularly valuable in environments where users' roles and responsibilities frequently change, or where access needs to be adjusted based on real-time conditions. For example, in a healthcare setting, PBAC can ensure that a doctor has access to patient records only when they are on duty and actively involved in the patient's care, while restricting access outside of these conditions.

Another advantage of PBAC is its alignment with regulatory compliance and data governance requirements. Many industries are subject to strict regulations regarding data privacy and access control, such as the General Data Protection Regulation (GDPR) and the Health Insurance Portability and Accountability Act (HIPAA). PBAC allows organizations to define and enforce policies that comply with these regulations, ensuring that sensitive data is accessed only by authorized individuals under appropriate conditions. Additionally, PBAC's centralized policy management and auditing capabilities make it easier to demonstrate compliance during regulatory inspections or audits.

PBAC also enhances security by minimizing the risk of over-permissioning and insider threats. In traditional access control models, users are often granted broad permissions based on their roles, which can lead to unnecessary access to sensitive data. This over-permissioning increases the risk of accidental data exposure or malicious activity by insiders. PBAC addresses this issue by ensuring that access is granted only when specific conditions are met, reducing the likelihood of unauthorized actions. Furthermore, PBAC can incorporate real-time monitoring and anomaly detection to identify and respond to suspicious behavior, adding an additional layer of security.

Despite its many benefits, implementing PBAC is not without challenges. One of the primary challenges is the complexity of policy creation and management. Defining comprehensive and effective policies requires a deep understanding of the organization's access control needs, business processes, and regulatory requirements. Poorly designed policies can lead to unintended access denials or permissions, potentially disrupting business operations or exposing sensitive data. To address this, organizations must invest in robust policy management tools and processes, including regular policy reviews, testing, and auditing.

Another challenge is the integration of PBAC with existing systems and infrastructure. Many organizations have established identity management and access control frameworks, such as RBAC or Attribute-Based Access Control (ABAC). Integrating PBAC into these environments requires careful planning to ensure compatibility and avoid disruptions. This may involve mapping existing roles and attributes to policies, updating legacy systems to support policy-based access control, and training administrators and users on the new model.

Performance is another consideration when implementing PBAC. Because PBAC evaluates access requests dynamically based on multiple policies and contextual factors, it can introduce latency in high-traffic environments. Ensuring that the PDP and PEP components are optimized for performance is essential to maintaining a seamless user experience. This might involve caching frequently used policies, distributing policy evaluation across multiple servers, or employing efficient decision-making algorithms.

The adoption of PBAC is growing as organizations recognize its potential to address the complexities of modern access control. The rise of cloud computing, mobile workforces, and interconnected systems has created environments where traditional access control models struggle to keep pace. PBAC's ability to provide dynamic, context-aware access control makes it an ideal solution for these dynamic and distributed environments. In cloud environments, PBAC enables organizations to manage access across multiple cloud services and platforms using a unified set of policies and contextual factors. Cloud service providers, such as Amazon Web Services (AWS), Microsoft Azure, and Google Cloud, offer PBAC capabilities that allow organizations to define access control policies based on resource tags, user properties, and environmental conditions.

PBAC also plays a critical role in supporting data privacy and protection initiatives. As organizations face increasing pressure to safeguard personal data and comply with privacy regulations, PBAC provides a powerful tool for enforcing data access policies. By using policies to control who can access specific data and under what conditions, organizations can ensure that personal information is only accessible to authorized users and for legitimate purposes.

The future of PBAC is closely tied to advancements in artificial intelligence (AI) and machine learning (ML). By integrating AI and ML capabilities into PBAC systems, organizations can enhance policy creation, management, and enforcement. For example, machine learning algorithms can analyze user behavior and access patterns to identify anomalies, recommend policy adjustments, and detect potential security threats. AI-driven PBAC systems can also automate the process of policy refinement, reducing administrative effort and improving the accuracy of access control decisions.

Another emerging trend is the combination of PBAC with other access control models, such as RBAC and ABAC, to create hybrid solutions that leverage the strengths of each approach. While RBAC provides a straightforward framework for defining roles and permissions, and ABAC offers flexibility through attributes, PBAC adds a layer of dynamic, rule-based decision-making that enhances both models. By combining these models, organizations can achieve a balance between simplicity and flexibility, ensuring that their access control systems are both effective and adaptable.

Policy-Based Access Control represents a significant evolution in the way organizations manage access to digital resources. By leveraging dynamic, context-aware policies, PBAC offers a flexible, scalable, and secure approach to access control that can adapt to the complexities of modern IT environments. As organizations continue to embrace digital transformation, cloud computing, and data privacy initiatives, PBAC will play an increasingly important role in ensuring that access to sensitive information is managed effectively and securely. Through careful implementation, robust policy management, and ongoing integration with emerging technologies, PBAC provides a foundation for the next generation of access control solutions.

Zero Trust Architecture: Never Trust, Always Verify

In today's rapidly evolving digital landscape, traditional security models that rely on perimeter-based defenses are no longer sufficient to protect organizations from sophisticated cyber threats. The assumption that everything inside a network can be trusted while external elements are considered dangerous has proven to be an outdated and risky approach. With the rise of remote work, cloud computing, and increasingly complex IT environments, attackers have found new ways to exploit vulnerabilities, often bypassing traditional defenses. Zero Trust Architecture (ZTA) has emerged as a revolutionary security paradigm designed to address these challenges by fundamentally shifting the way organizations approach cybersecurity. The core principle of Zero Trust is simple yet powerful: never trust, always verify.

At its heart, Zero Trust Architecture operates on the belief that trust is a vulnerability. Instead of assuming that users, devices, or applications within the network are inherently safe, Zero Trust requires continuous verification of every request, regardless of its origin. This means that no user or device is granted access by default, whether they are inside or outside the organization's network perimeter. Every access request must be authenticated, authorized, and encrypted, with strict adherence to the principle of least privilege, ensuring that users have only the permissions necessary to perform their tasks.

One of the foundational components of Zero Trust is strong identity verification. Identity and Access Management (IAM) systems play a critical role in ensuring that only authenticated users can access resources. Multi-Factor Authentication (MFA) is a standard feature in Zero Trust environments, requiring users to provide multiple forms of verification before gaining access. This could include something the user knows (a password), something the user has (a security token or smartphone), and something the user is (biometric data like a fingerprint or facial recognition). By layering these authentication methods, organizations can significantly reduce the risk of unauthorized access due to compromised credentials.

However, Zero Trust extends far beyond user authentication. It also encompasses device security, ensuring that only trusted devices can access the network. This involves continuously monitoring the health and compliance status of devices, checking for up-to-date software, security patches, and configurations. Devices that do not meet security standards are either denied access or granted limited access to prevent potential threats from spreading within the network. This approach, often referred to as device posture assessment, ensures that both the user and the device are trustworthy before access is granted.

Micro-segmentation is another key element of Zero Trust Architecture. Traditional networks often operate on a flat structure, where once an attacker gains access to the network, they can move laterally with relative ease, accessing sensitive data and systems. Micro-segmentation addresses this vulnerability by dividing the network into smaller, isolated segments, each with its own set of access controls and security policies. This means that even if an attacker breaches one segment, they cannot easily move to others without encountering additional layers of verification and defense. By limiting lateral movement, micro-segmentation significantly reduces the potential damage of a security breach.

In a Zero Trust environment, continuous monitoring and real-time analytics are essential for maintaining security. Security Information and Event Management (SIEM) systems, along with advanced threat detection tools powered by artificial intelligence (AI) and machine learning (ML), play a crucial role in identifying and responding to anomalies. These systems collect and analyze data from various sources, including network traffic, user behavior, and device activity, to detect suspicious patterns that may indicate a security threat. When anomalies are detected, automated responses can be triggered to isolate affected systems, revoke access, or alert security teams for further investigation.

Zero Trust also emphasizes the importance of data security and encryption. In traditional models, data is often protected primarily at the perimeter, but within the network, it may be left exposed. Zero Trust requires that data be encrypted both in transit and at rest, ensuring that even if it is intercepted or accessed by unauthorized users, it remains unreadable and secure. Data classification and labeling further enhance security by applying appropriate protection measures based on the sensitivity of the information. For example, highly confidential data may require stricter access controls and more robust encryption compared to less sensitive information.

The shift to cloud computing and remote work has accelerated the adoption of Zero Trust principles. In cloud environments, the traditional network perimeter no longer exists, and resources are often distributed across multiple platforms and services. Zero Trust provides a framework for securing these environments by applying consistent security policies and access controls regardless of where resources are located. Cloud service providers, such as Microsoft Azure, Amazon Web Services (AWS), and Google Cloud, have integrated Zero Trust features into their platforms, allowing organizations to manage access, monitor activity, and enforce security policies across hybrid and multi-cloud environments.

Implementing Zero Trust Architecture is not a one-size-fits-all approach, nor is it a solution that can be deployed overnight. It requires a comprehensive strategy that encompasses people, processes, and technology. Organizations must start by assessing their current security posture, identifying critical assets, and understanding the flow of data within their environments. From there, they can develop a roadmap for implementing Zero Trust principles, prioritizing areas of greatest risk and gradually extending protections across the organization.

One of the common misconceptions about Zero Trust is that it is overly restrictive and can hinder productivity. In reality, when implemented effectively, Zero Trust can enhance both security and user experience. By leveraging technologies such as Single Sign-On (SSO) and adaptive authentication, organizations can streamline access while maintaining strong security controls. Adaptive authentication, for example, adjusts the level of verification required based on the context of the access request. A user accessing resources from a trusted device and location may face fewer authentication steps, while an unusual login attempt from an unfamiliar location triggers additional verification measures.

Zero Trust also aligns with regulatory compliance and data protection requirements. Regulations such as the General Data Protection

Regulation (GDPR), the Health Insurance Portability and Accountability Act (HIPAA), and the Payment Card Industry Data Security Standard (PCI DSS) emphasize the need for strong access controls, data protection, and continuous monitoring. By adopting Zero Trust principles, organizations can more effectively meet these requirements, demonstrating a proactive approach to cybersecurity and reducing the risk of non-compliance penalties.

Despite its many advantages, the transition to Zero Trust Architecture can be challenging. It requires a cultural shift within organizations, as employees and stakeholders must adapt to new security practices and mindsets. Resistance to change, particularly when it comes to security measures that may be perceived as burdensome, can hinder implementation efforts. To overcome these challenges, organizations must prioritize communication and education, helping users understand the importance of Zero Trust and how it protects both the organization and individual users from security threats.

Technology integration is another critical factor in the success of Zero Trust initiatives. Organizations often rely on a diverse array of security tools and technologies, from identity management and endpoint protection to network monitoring and data encryption. Ensuring that these tools work together seamlessly to support Zero Trust principles requires careful planning and coordination. Many vendors now offer integrated Zero Trust solutions that simplify deployment and management, but organizations must still tailor these solutions to their specific needs and environments.

The future of Zero Trust Architecture is closely tied to advancements in technology and the evolving threat landscape. As cyber threats continue to grow in sophistication, Zero Trust provides a resilient framework that can adapt to new challenges. Emerging technologies such as artificial intelligence, machine learning, and behavioral analytics will further enhance Zero Trust capabilities, enabling organizations to detect and respond to threats with greater speed and accuracy. Additionally, the rise of the Internet of Things (IoT) and edge computing presents new opportunities and challenges for Zero Trust, as organizations must secure an expanding array of devices and data sources.

Zero Trust Architecture represents a fundamental shift in how organizations approach cybersecurity. By eliminating implicit trust and requiring continuous verification, Zero Trust provides a robust and adaptable framework for protecting digital assets in an increasingly complex and dynamic world. While the journey to Zero Trust may be challenging, the benefits in terms of enhanced security, compliance, and resilience make it a vital strategy for any organization committed to safeguarding its data and systems in the digital age.

Passwordless Authentication: The New Standard?

In the realm of digital security, passwords have long been the default mechanism for verifying identity. Since the dawn of the internet, users have relied on alphanumeric strings to protect their accounts, data, and online activities. However, as technology has advanced, so have the methods for compromising these traditional security measures. Passwords, once considered robust, are increasingly viewed as a weak link in the cybersecurity chain. The rise of phishing attacks, credential stuffing, brute-force attacks, and the simple human tendency to reuse or forget passwords have all contributed to the vulnerabilities inherent in password-based systems. As organizations and individuals grapple with these security challenges, passwordless authentication is emerging as a compelling alternative, promising both enhanced security and a more seamless user experience.

Passwordless authentication refers to methods of verifying a user's identity without the need for a traditional password. Instead of relying on something the user knows—a password or PIN—passwordless systems leverage factors such as biometrics, hardware tokens, or cryptographic keys. These methods are inherently more secure because they eliminate the risks associated with password theft, reuse, and phishing. In addition to bolstering security, passwordless authentication simplifies the login process, reducing friction for users and minimizing the frustration associated with forgotten credentials.

One of the most common forms of passwordless authentication is biometric verification. Technologies such as fingerprint scanning, facial recognition, and iris scanning have become ubiquitous, particularly with the widespread adoption of smartphones equipped with biometric sensors. Apple's Touch ID and Face ID, as well as similar features on Android devices, have made biometric authentication a familiar and trusted method for millions of users worldwide. Biometrics offer a high level of security because they rely on unique, immutable physical characteristics that are difficult to replicate or steal. Unlike passwords, which can be guessed or leaked, biometric data is tied directly to the individual, providing a strong assurance of identity.

Another prevalent approach to passwordless authentication involves the use of hardware tokens or security keys. Devices like YubiKeys and other FIDO2-compliant tokens generate cryptographic keys that are used to authenticate the user. These hardware-based solutions provide an extra layer of security by ensuring that only someone in physical possession of the token can gain access to an account or system. Because the authentication process relies on cryptographic principles, it is resistant to common attacks like phishing or man-in-the-middle attacks. Even if an attacker obtains the user's login credentials, they cannot access the account without the physical token.

Mobile-based authentication is also gaining traction as a passwordless solution. This method leverages smartphones as secure authentication devices, using features like push notifications, one-time passwords (OTPs), or QR codes to verify identity. For example, when a user attempts to log into an application, they receive a push notification on their registered mobile device, prompting them to approve or deny the login attempt. This process ensures that only the legitimate user, who has access to the registered device, can complete the authentication. Mobile-based authentication combines convenience with security, as most users already carry their smartphones and are familiar with managing app-based notifications.

Public key infrastructure (PKI) and cryptographic keys are foundational to many passwordless authentication systems. In a PKI-based system, each user has a pair of cryptographic keys: a public key, which is shared with the authentication server, and a private key, which remains securely stored on the user's device. When the user attempts to authenticate, the server sends a challenge that can only be correctly answered using the private key. This challenge-response mechanism ensures that the user possesses the private key without transmitting sensitive information over the network. Because the private key never leaves the user's device, it is protected from interception and theft.

The benefits of passwordless authentication extend beyond security. One of the most significant advantages is the improvement in user experience. Password fatigue—the frustration associated with managing multiple complex passwords—is a common issue for users in both personal and professional contexts. Passwordless systems eliminate the need to remember or manage passwords, streamlining the login process and reducing cognitive load. This ease of use can lead to increased user satisfaction, higher adoption rates, and improved productivity, particularly in workplace environments where employees access multiple applications and systems daily.

Passwordless authentication also reduces the administrative burden on IT departments. Managing password resets and recovery processes is a time-consuming and costly task for support teams. Forgotten passwords are among the most common reasons for help desk calls, leading to lost productivity and increased operational costs. By eliminating passwords, organizations can significantly reduce the volume of support requests related to login issues, freeing up resources to focus on more strategic initiatives. Additionally, passwordless systems simplify compliance with security policies and regulatory requirements, as they inherently mitigate risks associated with weak or compromised passwords.

Despite its many advantages, the transition to passwordless authentication is not without challenges. One of the primary concerns is the initial implementation and integration with existing systems. Many organizations have legacy applications and infrastructure that were designed around traditional password-based authentication. Migrating to passwordless solutions requires careful planning, investment in new technologies, and potentially significant changes to the IT environment. Ensuring compatibility with various platforms, devices, and user workflows can be complex, particularly in large or highly regulated organizations.

Another challenge is user acceptance and trust. While passwordless authentication offers clear security and usability benefits, some users may be hesitant to adopt new methods, particularly if they are unfamiliar with technologies like biometrics or hardware tokens. Concerns about privacy and data security, especially regarding the storage and use of biometric data, can also hinder adoption. Organizations must address these concerns through clear communication, user education, and transparent policies that emphasize the security and privacy protections in place.

Security considerations are paramount in passwordless authentication systems. While eliminating passwords reduces many common attack vectors, it introduces new risks that must be managed. For example, biometric data, if compromised, cannot be changed like a password. Ensuring that biometric data is securely stored and processed, often in secure enclaves or on-device storage, is critical to maintaining user trust and system integrity. Similarly, the loss or theft of hardware tokens or mobile devices can pose risks if not mitigated through multi-factor authentication or robust recovery processes.

The future of passwordless authentication is closely tied to the development and adoption of standards such as FIDO2 and WebAuthn. These standards, developed by the FIDO Alliance and the World Wide Web Consortium (W3C), provide a framework for secure, interoperable passwordless authentication across different devices and platforms. By leveraging public key cryptography and hardware-based security, FIDO2 and WebAuthn enable strong, phishing-resistant authentication for web applications, enterprise systems, and consumer services. As these standards gain traction, they are expected to drive broader adoption of passwordless solutions, fostering a more secure and user-friendly digital ecosystem.

Emerging technologies, such as decentralized identity and blockchain, also hold promise for the evolution of passwordless authentication. Decentralized identity systems give users control over their own credentials, allowing them to authenticate securely without relying on centralized authorities. By combining passwordless authentication with decentralized identity, users can benefit from enhanced privacy, security, and autonomy over their digital identities. Blockchain technology can further enhance these systems by providing immutable, tamper-resistant records of authentication events and credential management.

Artificial intelligence and machine learning are also playing a role in advancing passwordless authentication. These technologies can be used to analyze user behavior, detect anomalies, and enhance security by identifying suspicious activities in real-time. Behavioral biometrics, which analyze patterns in how users interact with devices—such as typing speed, mouse movements, or touchscreen gestures—offer an additional layer of security that complements traditional biometrics and cryptographic methods. By continuously monitoring and adapting to user behavior, AI-driven systems can provide dynamic, context-aware authentication that balances security with usability.

Passwordless authentication is rapidly gaining momentum as organizations seek to enhance security, improve user experience, and reduce the operational burdens associated with password management. While challenges remain in terms of implementation, user adoption, and security considerations, the benefits of passwordless systems are compelling. As technology continues to evolve and standards like FIDO2 and WebAuthn become more widespread, passwordless authentication is poised to become the new standard for digital identity verification. By embracing this shift, organizations can create a more secure, efficient, and user-friendly digital environment, paving the way for the future of authentication in an increasingly connected world.

Session Management and Security

In the digital age, where web applications and online services have become integral to both personal and professional life, session management plays a critical role in maintaining security and user experience. Sessions are temporary interactions between a user and an application, allowing users to stay logged in while performing various tasks without re-authenticating for each action. However, while sessions offer convenience and seamless interaction, they also introduce significant security risks if not managed properly. The ability to secure these sessions is fundamental to protecting user data, preventing unauthorized access, and ensuring the integrity of online services.

Session management refers to the process of establishing, maintaining, and terminating a session between a user and a service. When a user logs into an application, the system generates a unique session identifier (session ID) that keeps track of the user's activities and access rights. This session ID is typically stored on the client side in cookies, URL parameters, or local storage, and it is sent to the server with each request to authenticate the session. The server, in turn, uses the session ID to recognize the user and maintain continuity across multiple interactions. While this process is essential for user convenience, it also presents potential vulnerabilities if session IDs are exposed or improperly handled.

One of the most common security threats related to session management is session hijacking. This occurs when an attacker gains unauthorized access to a user's session ID and uses it to impersonate the user. There are several methods by which attackers can hijack sessions, including cross-site scripting (XSS), man-in-the-middle (MITM) attacks, and session fixation. In an XSS attack, malicious scripts are injected into a legitimate website, allowing attackers to steal session cookies from unsuspecting users. MITM attacks, on the other hand, involve intercepting communication between the user and the server, often over unsecured networks, to capture session IDs. Session fixation occurs when an attacker sets a known session ID for a user and waits for them to log in, thereby gaining unauthorized access to the authenticated session.

To mitigate these risks, robust session management practices must be implemented. One of the fundamental principles of secure session management is the use of strong, unpredictable session IDs. Session IDs should be generated using secure random number generators and should be long enough to prevent brute-force attacks. Additionally, session IDs should be unique for each session to prevent reuse and reduce the risk of session fixation attacks. Encrypting session data, both in transit and at rest, adds an extra layer of protection, ensuring that even if session IDs are intercepted, they cannot be easily exploited.

Another critical aspect of session security is the proper handling of session cookies. Cookies are the most common method of storing session IDs on the client side, and their security settings play a vital role in protecting sessions. The Secure flag should be set on cookies to ensure they are only transmitted over HTTPS connections, preventing interception over unsecured networks. The HttpOnly flag should be enabled to prevent client-side scripts from accessing session cookies, mitigating the risk of XSS attacks. Additionally, the SameSite attribute can be used to restrict the sending of cookies to the same site, reducing the risk of cross-site request forgery (CSRF) attacks.

Session expiration and timeout policies are also essential components of session management. Sessions should have a defined lifespan, automatically expiring after a certain period of inactivity or after a maximum duration. This limits the window of opportunity for attackers to hijack sessions and ensures that abandoned sessions do not remain active indefinitely. Implementing idle timeouts forces users to re-authenticate after a period of inactivity, while absolute timeouts terminate sessions after a set period, regardless of activity. These policies help balance security with user convenience, reducing the risk of unauthorized access while minimizing disruption to legitimate users.

In addition to time-based session management, organizations should implement mechanisms for actively managing and terminating sessions. Users should have the ability to log out of sessions manually, and logout processes should ensure that session IDs are invalidated on the server side. Simply removing session cookies from the client side is not sufficient, as this does not terminate the session on the server, leaving it vulnerable to hijacking. Implementing session revocation mechanisms, such as invalidating tokens or session IDs upon logout or password changes, further enhances security by ensuring that old sessions cannot be reused.

Multi-factor authentication (MFA) can also play a role in securing sessions. While MFA is typically associated with the initial login process, it can be extended to session management by requiring re-authentication for sensitive actions or after a certain period. For example, a banking application might require a user to enter a one-time password (OTP) before transferring large sums of money, even if the user is already logged in. This additional layer of verification helps protect against session hijacking and unauthorized actions, particularly in high-risk environments.

Monitoring and logging are critical for detecting and responding to session-related security incidents. Organizations should implement comprehensive logging of session activities, including login attempts, session creation, and session termination events. Anomalies, such as multiple concurrent sessions from different locations or devices, should trigger alerts for further investigation. Security Information and Event Management (SIEM) systems can aggregate and analyze session logs in real time, enabling organizations to identify suspicious behavior and respond promptly to potential threats.

With the rise of cloud computing and mobile applications, session management has become even more complex. Users frequently switch between devices and networks, creating challenges for maintaining secure sessions across diverse environments. Federated identity and single sign-on (SSO) solutions offer a way to streamline session management in these scenarios. By centralizing authentication and session management through trusted identity providers, organizations can ensure consistent security policies while providing users with a seamless experience across multiple applications and services. However, these solutions also introduce new risks, as compromising a single session or identity provider can potentially grant access to multiple systems. Therefore, securing federated sessions and ensuring strong identity provider security is paramount.

The adoption of stateless authentication mechanisms, such as JSON Web Tokens (JWT), has also influenced modern session management practices. Unlike traditional session management, where session state is maintained on the server, stateless authentication embeds session information within the token itself, which is passed between the client and server with each request. While this approach offers scalability and reduces server-side overhead, it also requires careful handling of token security. Tokens should be signed and encrypted to prevent tampering, and mechanisms for token revocation and expiration must be in place to ensure that compromised tokens cannot be reused.

Emerging technologies and trends continue to shape the future of session management and security. The rise of passwordless authentication, biometrics, and behavioral analytics offers new ways to verify user identity and secure sessions without relying on traditional credentials. For example, continuous authentication techniques use real-time analysis of user behavior, such as typing patterns or mouse movements, to verify identity throughout a session. This dynamic approach to session management enhances security by constantly assessing the legitimacy of the user, rather than relying solely on initial authentication.

Zero Trust Architecture (ZTA) principles are also influencing session management strategies. In a Zero Trust environment, no user or device is inherently trusted, and continuous verification is required for all access requests. This approach extends to session management, where every interaction is scrutinized, and access is granted based on real-time risk assessments. Implementing Zero Trust principles in session management involves integrating identity verification, device compliance checks, and contextual factors into the decision-making process, ensuring that sessions remain secure throughout their lifecycle.

Session management is a critical component of cybersecurity that directly impacts both security and user experience. By implementing robust session management practices, organizations can protect against session hijacking, unauthorized access, and data breaches, while providing users with seamless and secure interactions. As technology continues to evolve, so too must session management strategies, incorporating new tools, techniques, and frameworks to address emerging threats and challenges. Balancing security with usability, and ensuring that sessions are both secure and efficient, remains a fundamental goal in the ever-changing landscape of digital security.

The Impact of Social Logins on Identity Verification

As digital platforms multiply and online interactions become more intricate, managing multiple accounts and passwords has become a significant challenge for users. In response to this, social logins have emerged as a convenient solution, allowing users to access various services and websites using their existing credentials from popular social media platforms like Facebook, Google, Twitter, and LinkedIn. By simplifying the login process, social logins enhance user experience and reduce the friction associated with creating and managing numerous accounts. However, while social logins offer convenience, they also introduce new challenges and considerations for identity verification, privacy, and security.

Social logins rely on the principles of federated identity, where a third-party identity provider (IdP)—in this case, a social media platform—authenticates the user on behalf of the service provider (SP), such as an e-commerce site, a news outlet, or a productivity app. When a user chooses to log in using their social media credentials, they are redirected to the social platform's authentication page, where they enter their login details. Once authenticated, the social platform sends an authorization token back to the service provider, confirming the user's identity and granting access to the requested service. This process is typically facilitated by protocols like OAuth and OpenID Connect, which ensure secure communication between the identity provider and the service provider.

The primary advantage of social logins is the convenience they offer to users. Instead of remembering separate usernames and passwords for each website or application, users can rely on a single set of credentials from a trusted social platform. This not only simplifies the login process but also reduces the likelihood of password fatigue, where users resort to weak or reused passwords due to the difficulty of managing multiple accounts. By minimizing the need for new account creation, social logins also streamline the onboarding process for new users, leading to higher conversion rates and improved user retention for service providers.

For businesses and service providers, social logins offer additional benefits beyond user convenience. By leveraging social platforms for authentication, organizations can reduce the complexity and cost associated with managing their own identity verification systems. Instead of building and maintaining secure authentication infrastructure, businesses can rely on established platforms with robust security measures in place. This can be particularly advantageous for smaller companies or startups that lack the resources to develop comprehensive identity management solutions.

Moreover, social logins provide service providers with valuable user data that can be used to personalize experiences and improve engagement. When users authenticate through social platforms, they often grant permission for the service provider to access certain profile information, such as their name, email address, profile picture, and even friend lists or interests. This data can be used to tailor content, recommend products, or facilitate social features like sharing and connecting with friends. For marketers and developers, this rich source of user information offers opportunities to enhance user engagement and drive targeted marketing efforts.

However, the use of social logins also raises important concerns regarding privacy, security, and the integrity of identity verification. One of the primary issues is the centralization of identity data with a few dominant social platforms. When users rely on a single social login for multiple services, they effectively concentrate their digital identities with that platform. This creates a single point of failure, where a breach or compromise of the social media account can potentially grant unauthorized access to all connected services. If a user's Facebook or Google account is hacked, for example, the attacker could gain access to a wide range of other accounts, from online shopping to banking services.

Privacy concerns are also paramount when it comes to social logins. By using a social platform to authenticate, users often consent to sharing their personal data with third-party service providers. While some platforms allow users to control the scope of data shared, many users may not fully understand the implications of granting access to their information. This can lead to unintended exposure of personal data, such as contacts, location history, or browsing habits, raising questions about data ownership, consent, and transparency. Additionally, the aggregation of user data across multiple services increases the risk of profiling and targeted advertising, potentially infringing on user privacy.

From a security perspective, social logins can introduce vulnerabilities if not implemented correctly. Service providers must ensure that the OAuth and OpenID Connect protocols are properly configured to prevent common attacks such as token interception, cross-site request forgery (CSRF), and phishing. Inadequate implementation of these protocols can expose users to security risks, undermining the benefits of using trusted identity providers. Furthermore, service providers must establish robust mechanisms for session management, ensuring that authentication tokens are securely stored, transmitted, and revoked when necessary.

The reliance on social logins also poses challenges for identity verification in contexts where strong assurance of identity is required. While social platforms can provide a convenient means of authentication, they do not always offer the level of identity verification needed for sensitive transactions, such as financial services, healthcare, or government applications. Social media accounts are relatively easy to create and can be anonymous or pseudonymous, making them unsuitable for situations that require verified, legal identities. In such cases, additional identity verification measures, such as multi-factor authentication, biometric verification, or integration with government-issued IDs, may be necessary to ensure the integrity of the authentication process.

Despite these challenges, social logins continue to evolve and adapt to the changing landscape of digital identity verification. Major social platforms have introduced enhanced security features, such as two-factor authentication (2FA) and login alerts, to protect user accounts from unauthorized access. Additionally, efforts are being made to improve transparency and user control over data sharing, allowing users to review and manage the permissions granted to third-party services. These developments aim to address some of the privacy and security concerns associated with social logins while maintaining their convenience and ease of use.

The rise of decentralized identity systems presents an interesting counterpoint to the dominance of social logins. Decentralized identity solutions aim to give users greater control over their digital identities by allowing them to manage their credentials independently of centralized platforms. Using technologies like blockchain and cryptographic proofs, decentralized identity systems enable users to authenticate securely without relying on a single identity provider. While still in their early stages, these systems offer a promising alternative to social logins, emphasizing privacy, security, and user sovereignty.

Another emerging trend is the integration of passwordless authentication methods with social logins. By combining the convenience of social logins with the security of passwordless technologies, such as biometrics or hardware tokens, service providers can offer a more robust and user-friendly authentication experience. For example, a user might authenticate with their Google account using a biometric scan on their smartphone, eliminating the need for passwords while leveraging the security infrastructure of a trusted identity provider. This hybrid approach balances the benefits of social logins with the need for stronger security measures.

As the digital ecosystem continues to expand, the role of social logins in identity verification will likely remain significant. Their ability to simplify access and improve user experience makes them an attractive option for both users and service providers. However, balancing convenience with security and privacy remains a critical challenge. Organizations must carefully consider the implications of integrating social logins into their systems, ensuring that they implement best practices for secure authentication while respecting user privacy and data protection.

The impact of social logins on identity verification reflects broader trends in the evolution of digital identity. As technology advances and user expectations shift, the need for secure, user-friendly authentication solutions will continue to drive innovation in this space. Whether through enhanced social login mechanisms, decentralized identity systems, or passwordless technologies, the future of identity verification will be shaped by the ongoing quest to balance convenience, security, and privacy in an increasingly connected world.

Privileged Access Management (PAM): Protecting the Keys to the Kingdom

In the complex world of modern IT environments, where organizations rely on vast networks, cloud services, and interconnected systems, privileged accounts represent one of the most significant security risks. These accounts, often held by system administrators, IT managers, and other high-level users, have elevated access rights that allow them to control critical infrastructure, manage sensitive data, and configure system-wide settings. Because of the power and reach of these accounts, they are often referred to as the "keys to the kingdom." If compromised, privileged accounts can give attackers unrestricted access to an organization's most valuable assets, leading to data breaches, operational disruptions, and significant financial and reputational damage. Privileged Access Management (PAM) is a specialized area of cybersecurity designed to address this risk by securing, monitoring, and controlling privileged accounts.

Privileged Access Management is a framework of policies, technologies, and processes that ensure only authorized individuals have access to sensitive systems and data, and only when necessary. PAM solutions are designed to enforce the principle of least privilege, granting users the minimum level of access required to perform their job functions. This reduces the attack surface by limiting the number of accounts with broad access rights and tightly controlling how these accounts are used. PAM also provides visibility and oversight into privileged activities, allowing organizations to detect and respond to suspicious behavior before it can cause harm.

One of the core components of PAM is the secure management of privileged credentials. Unlike standard user accounts, privileged accounts often have access to administrative functions, databases, servers, and network devices. These accounts are attractive targets for attackers seeking to escalate their privileges and gain deeper access to an organization's infrastructure. PAM solutions typically include a secure vault for storing and managing privileged credentials, ensuring they are encrypted and protected from unauthorized access. This vault serves as a central repository where passwords, SSH keys, and other sensitive credentials are stored, rotated regularly, and accessed only by authorized users through controlled mechanisms.

Password management is a critical aspect of PAM. Many data breaches occur because of weak, reused, or improperly stored passwords. PAM systems automate the process of rotating and updating privileged credentials, reducing the risk of credential theft and ensuring that passwords meet organizational security standards. By eliminating hard-coded credentials in scripts and applications, PAM helps prevent attackers from exploiting known vulnerabilities. Automated password rotation also ensures that even if a password is compromised, it will only be valid for a short period, limiting the window of opportunity for attackers.

Another essential feature of PAM is session management and monitoring. Privileged sessions—interactions where users perform administrative tasks—are closely monitored and recorded to ensure accountability and detect suspicious activity. PAM solutions often provide real-time session monitoring, allowing security teams to observe privileged activities as they occur and intervene if necessary. These sessions are typically recorded in video or text formats, creating an audit trail that can be reviewed later for compliance purposes or forensic analysis in the event of a security incident. By maintaining a detailed record of who accessed what, when, and for what purpose, PAM enhances transparency and accountability within the organization.

Just-in-time (JIT) access is another advanced feature offered by PAM solutions. Instead of granting permanent privileged access to users, JIT access provides temporary, time-bound privileges that expire after the task is completed. This minimizes the risk associated with standing privileged accounts, which can become targets for attackers if left active and unmanaged. By granting access only when needed and for the shortest possible duration, JIT access reduces the likelihood of misuse or unauthorized access.

Privileged Access Management also plays a vital role in enforcing multi-factor authentication (MFA) for privileged accounts. Given the high level of risk associated with these accounts, relying on passwords alone is insufficient. PAM solutions integrate with MFA technologies to require additional forms of verification, such as biometric data, hardware tokens, or one-time passwords (OTPs), before granting access to privileged accounts. This additional layer of security ensures that even if credentials are compromised, unauthorized users cannot easily gain access.

The importance of PAM extends beyond internal threats to include third-party vendors and contractors who require temporary access to an organization's systems. Third-party access is a common source of security vulnerabilities, as external users may not adhere to the same security practices as internal staff. PAM solutions provide secure mechanisms for managing third-party access, including credential management, session monitoring, and time-limited privileges. By applying the same rigorous controls to external users, organizations can mitigate the risks associated with vendor access and maintain a consistent security posture across all privileged activities.

Compliance with regulatory requirements is another driving factor behind the adoption of PAM solutions. Many industries are subject to strict regulations regarding data protection, access control, and auditing, such as the General Data Protection Regulation (GDPR), the Health Insurance Portability and Accountability Act (HIPAA), and the Sarbanes-Oxley Act (SOX). PAM provides the tools and processes necessary to meet these requirements, including detailed audit logs, access control policies, and regular reporting. By demonstrating control over privileged access, organizations can ensure compliance with legal standards and reduce the risk of penalties or legal actions resulting from data breaches.

Despite its many benefits, implementing Privileged Access Management is not without challenges. One of the primary obstacles is the complexity of integrating PAM into existing IT environments. Organizations often have a wide range of systems, applications, and devices, each with its own access control mechanisms. Ensuring that PAM solutions can manage and monitor privileged access across this diverse landscape requires careful planning, customization, and ongoing maintenance. Additionally, organizations must balance security with usability, ensuring that PAM controls do not hinder productivity or create friction for legitimate users.

User resistance is another common challenge when implementing PAM. Employees, particularly IT staff and administrators, may be accustomed to having broad access rights and may view PAM controls as restrictive or burdensome. To overcome this resistance, organizations must emphasize the importance of PAM in protecting both the organization and its employees from security threats. Providing training and clear communication about how PAM enhances security without compromising efficiency can help foster a culture of security awareness and cooperation.

The future of Privileged Access Management is closely tied to emerging technologies and evolving cybersecurity threats. As organizations increasingly adopt cloud computing, PAM solutions must adapt to manage privileged access in hybrid and multi-cloud environments. Cloud-native PAM tools offer scalable, flexible solutions for securing cloud infrastructure, integrating with cloud service providers' native security features, and providing consistent controls across on-premises and cloud environments.

Artificial intelligence (AI) and machine learning (ML) are also shaping the future of PAM by enabling more sophisticated monitoring and threat detection. AI-driven PAM solutions can analyze patterns of privileged activity, identify anomalies, and predict potential security incidents before they occur. For example, if an administrator accesses sensitive systems at an unusual time or from an unfamiliar location, the PAM system can trigger alerts or automatically revoke access to prevent potential breaches. These intelligent capabilities enhance the effectiveness of PAM by enabling proactive security measures and reducing the reliance on manual oversight.

Privileged Access Management is a critical component of modern cybersecurity strategies, protecting the most sensitive assets and systems within an organization. By securing privileged credentials, monitoring privileged activities, and enforcing strict access controls, PAM reduces the risk of data breaches, insider threats, and compliance violations. As technology continues to evolve and cyber threats become more sophisticated, PAM will remain an essential tool for safeguarding the "keys to the kingdom" and ensuring the integrity, confidentiality, and availability of organizational resources. Through continuous improvement, integration with emerging technologies, and a commitment to security best practices, PAM provides a robust foundation for managing privileged access in an increasingly complex digital world.

Identity Lifecycle Management: From Onboarding to Offboarding

In today's interconnected digital world, organizations must manage the identities of employees, contractors, partners, and even devices to ensure secure access to systems and data. Identity Lifecycle Management (ILM) is the comprehensive process that governs the creation, maintenance, and eventual deactivation of these identities throughout their relationship with an organization. From onboarding a new employee to offboarding a departing one, ILM ensures that identities are managed consistently and securely, aligning access permissions with organizational policies and regulatory requirements.

The identity lifecycle begins with onboarding, the process of creating a digital identity for a new user. This step is critical, as it establishes the foundation for all future interactions between the user and the organization's systems. During onboarding, identity management systems capture key information about the user, such as their name, job title, department, and contact details. This data is used to generate unique credentials—typically a username and initial password—that the user will use to access organizational resources. In many cases, onboarding also includes provisioning access to specific systems, applications, and data based on the user's role within the organization.

Automating the onboarding process is essential for ensuring efficiency, accuracy, and security. Identity and Access Management (IAM) solutions can streamline onboarding by integrating with human resources (HR) systems to automatically create user accounts when a new employee is hired. This automation reduces the administrative burden on IT teams and minimizes the risk of errors, such as assigning incorrect permissions or failing to create necessary accounts. Role-based access control (RBAC) is often used during onboarding to assign predefined sets of permissions based on the user's role, ensuring that they have the appropriate level of access from day one.

Once a user is onboarded, their identity must be maintained and managed throughout their tenure with the organization. This ongoing process includes updating personal information, modifying access permissions as roles change, and ensuring compliance with security policies. As employees move between departments, take on new responsibilities, or receive promotions, their access needs may evolve. Identity Lifecycle Management ensures that these changes are reflected in real-time, preventing privilege creep—where users accumulate excessive permissions over time—and reducing the risk of unauthorized access.

A key component of identity maintenance is the implementation of periodic access reviews and audits. Regularly reviewing user access rights helps organizations identify and address discrepancies, such as users retaining access to systems they no longer need or former employees whose accounts were not properly deactivated. Automated tools can facilitate these reviews by generating reports on user permissions and highlighting anomalies for further investigation. In addition to enhancing security, access reviews are often required to meet regulatory compliance standards, such as the General Data Protection Regulation (GDPR) or the Sarbanes-Oxley Act (SOX).

Another important aspect of identity management during the lifecycle is the application of multi-factor authentication (MFA) and other security measures to protect user accounts. As cyber threats become more sophisticated, relying solely on passwords is no longer sufficient to safeguard sensitive information. Implementing MFA adds an additional layer of security by requiring users to verify their identity using multiple factors, such as a password and a fingerprint scan or a one-time code sent to their mobile device. This approach significantly reduces the risk of unauthorized access, even if a user's credentials are compromised.

Identity Lifecycle Management also encompasses the management of temporary and external users, such as contractors, vendors, and partners. These users often require limited access to specific systems for a defined period. ILM ensures that temporary access is granted appropriately and that permissions are automatically revoked when they are no longer needed. This is particularly important in preventing unauthorized access by former contractors or external partners who no longer have a legitimate relationship with the organization. Just-in-time (JIT) access provisioning can further enhance security by granting temporary privileges only when necessary and automatically revoking them after a task is completed.

The final stage of the identity lifecycle is offboarding, the process of deactivating a user's identity when they leave the organization. Offboarding is a critical step in preventing security breaches and protecting sensitive data. If not handled properly, former employees may retain access to organizational systems, posing a significant risk of data theft, sabotage, or accidental exposure. Effective offboarding involves disabling user accounts, revoking access to all systems and applications, and recovering any organizational assets, such as laptops, security tokens, or mobile devices.

Automating the offboarding process is essential for ensuring that no access points are overlooked. IAM solutions can integrate with HR systems to trigger automatic deactivation of user accounts when an employee's departure is recorded. This automation ensures that access is revoked promptly, reducing the risk of unauthorized activity. Additionally, organizations should implement processes for recovering and securing data associated with departing employees, such as transferring ownership of files and emails to other team members or archiving data for future reference.

In addition to technical measures, offboarding should include administrative steps, such as conducting exit interviews and reminding departing employees of their ongoing obligations regarding confidentiality and data protection. These steps help reinforce the importance of security and can provide valuable insights into potential vulnerabilities or areas for improvement in the identity management process.

Identity Lifecycle Management is not limited to human users; it also extends to devices, applications, and services that interact with organizational systems. As the Internet of Things (IoT) and machine-to-machine (M2M) communications become more prevalent, managing the identities of non-human entities is increasingly important. ILM ensures that devices are properly authenticated, authorized, and monitored throughout their lifecycle, from initial deployment to decommissioning. This approach helps protect against unauthorized access, data breaches, and other security threats associated with connected devices.

The adoption of cloud computing and hybrid IT environments has added complexity to Identity Lifecycle Management. Users now access systems and data from various locations, devices, and networks, making it essential to manage identities consistently across on-premises and cloud-based environments. Cloud Identity and Access Management (CIAM) solutions provide centralized control over user identities, enabling organizations to apply consistent policies and security measures regardless of where resources are located. CIAM also supports federated identity and single sign-on (SSO) capabilities, allowing users to access multiple applications with a single set of credentials while maintaining strong security controls.

Regulatory compliance is a significant driver of Identity Lifecycle Management practices. Organizations must adhere to various legal and industry-specific requirements that dictate how personal data is collected, stored, and accessed. For example, the GDPR mandates that organizations implement appropriate technical and organizational measures to protect personal data and ensure that access is granted only to authorized individuals. ILM solutions help organizations meet these requirements by providing tools for access control, auditing, and reporting, ensuring that identities are managed in accordance with legal standards.

Emerging technologies, such as artificial intelligence (AI) and machine learning (ML), are also transforming Identity Lifecycle Management. AI-driven ILM solutions can analyze user behavior, detect anomalies, and automate decision-making processes related to access control. For example, if an employee suddenly attempts to access sensitive data outside of their usual working hours or from an unfamiliar location, the ILM system can flag the activity for review or automatically trigger additional authentication requirements. These intelligent capabilities enhance security by enabling proactive detection and response to potential threats.

As organizations continue to embrace digital transformation, the importance of Identity Lifecycle Management will only grow. Managing identities effectively is essential for protecting sensitive data, ensuring regulatory compliance, and maintaining operational efficiency. By automating key processes, implementing robust security measures, and integrating with emerging technologies, organizations can build a comprehensive ILM framework that supports their evolving needs. Ultimately, Identity Lifecycle Management is about more than just managing user accounts; it is a critical component of a broader cybersecurity strategy that safeguards the integrity, confidentiality, and availability of organizational resources throughout the entire lifecycle of every identity.

Identity Governance and Administration (IGA): Ensuring Compliance

In today's digital landscape, where organizations manage vast amounts of sensitive data and operate within increasingly complex IT environments, identity management is not just about granting access—it's also about ensuring that the right people have the right access to the right resources at the right time. This delicate balance between accessibility and security is at the heart of Identity Governance and Administration (IGA). IGA goes beyond basic identity and access management (IAM) by incorporating policies, processes, and tools that help organizations not only control who has access to what but also ensure that this access complies with internal policies and external regulations.

At its core, Identity Governance and Administration is about visibility and control. It provides organizations with the ability to see who has access to their systems and data, how that access was granted, and whether it aligns with organizational policies and regulatory requirements. This visibility is crucial in preventing unauthorized access, reducing the risk of data breaches, and ensuring compliance with laws such as the General Data Protection Regulation (GDPR), the Sarbanes-Oxley Act (SOX), and the Health Insurance Portability and Accountability Act (HIPAA).

One of the fundamental components of IGA is access certification, also known as attestation. This process involves regularly reviewing and validating user access rights to ensure they are appropriate and necessary. Access certification helps prevent privilege creep, where users accumulate access rights over time that exceed their current job requirements. By requiring managers or data owners to periodically review and approve access permissions, organizations can maintain a clean and secure access environment. This not only enhances security but also demonstrates due diligence in adhering to compliance requirements.

Role management is another critical aspect of IGA. In many organizations, access is granted based on roles, which are collections of permissions that correspond to specific job functions. IGA solutions help define, manage, and optimize these roles to ensure they accurately reflect organizational needs. Role mining and role engineering are techniques used to analyze existing access patterns and create efficient, least-privilege roles. By aligning roles with business functions, organizations can streamline access provisioning, reduce administrative overhead, and minimize the risk of over-permissioning.

Policy enforcement is central to the effectiveness of IGA. Organizations must establish clear policies that govern how identities are managed, how access is granted, and how compliance is maintained. These policies might include rules about password complexity, multi-factor authentication (MFA), segregation of duties (SoD), and data access limitations. Segregation of duties, in particular, is a key compliance requirement that ensures no single individual has conflicting responsibilities that could lead to fraud or errors. For example, in a financial setting, the person who approves expenses should not be the same person who processes payments. IGA solutions automate the enforcement of these policies, ensuring that violations are detected and addressed promptly.

Provisioning and de-provisioning are also essential components of IGA. Provisioning refers to the process of creating user accounts and granting access to resources when a new employee joins the organization or when an existing employee takes on new responsibilities. De-provisioning, on the other hand, involves revoking access when an employee leaves the organization or no longer requires certain permissions. Automated provisioning and de-provisioning processes ensure that access rights are granted and removed promptly and accurately, reducing the risk of unauthorized access and improving operational efficiency.

Audit and reporting capabilities are critical for maintaining compliance and demonstrating accountability. IGA solutions provide detailed logs and reports that track user activities, access changes, and policy violations. These reports can be used to conduct internal audits, respond to external regulatory inquiries, and identify potential security issues. Regular auditing helps organizations maintain a continuous state of compliance and quickly address any discrepancies or vulnerabilities that arise.

The integration of IGA with other IT systems enhances its effectiveness and provides a more comprehensive view of identity and access management across the organization. For example, integrating IGA with human resources (HR) systems allows for seamless onboarding and offboarding, ensuring that user access aligns with employment status and role changes. Integration with security information and event management (SIEM) systems enables real-time monitoring and analysis of identity-related activities, helping detect and respond to suspicious behavior.

As organizations increasingly adopt cloud services and hybrid IT environments, the scope of IGA must expand to cover these new landscapes. Cloud Identity Governance extends traditional IGA capabilities to cloud applications and services, ensuring consistent access controls and compliance across on-premises and cloud environments. This is particularly important as organizations use multiple cloud providers and software-as-a-service (SaaS) applications, each with its own access management systems. Unified IGA solutions provide a centralized approach to managing identities and access across these diverse platforms.

Regulatory compliance is a significant driver of IGA adoption. Many industries are subject to strict data protection and privacy regulations that require organizations to implement robust identity and access controls. For example, GDPR mandates that organizations protect personal data and ensure that access is limited to authorized individuals. SOX requires stringent controls over financial reporting processes, including access to financial systems and data. HIPAA sets standards for protecting sensitive health information, including who can access patient records and under what circumstances. IGA solutions help organizations meet these regulatory requirements by providing tools for access control, policy enforcement, auditing, and reporting.

The role of IGA in risk management cannot be overstated. By providing visibility into who has access to critical systems and data, IGA helps organizations identify potential security risks and take proactive measures to mitigate them. This includes detecting and addressing issues such as orphaned accounts (accounts that remain active after an employee leaves), excessive permissions, and policy violations. Risk-based access controls, which adjust access rights based on the user's risk profile and behavior, further enhance security and compliance efforts.

Artificial intelligence (AI) and machine learning (ML) are increasingly being integrated into IGA solutions to enhance their capabilities. AI-driven IGA systems can analyze large volumes of identity and access data to identify patterns, detect anomalies, and predict potential security threats. For example, if an employee suddenly accesses a large number of sensitive files outside of normal working hours, the IGA system can flag this behavior as suspicious and trigger an investigation. Machine learning algorithms can also help optimize role management by identifying the most efficient role structures based on actual usage patterns.

User behavior analytics (UBA) is another emerging technology that complements IGA by providing deeper insights into how users interact with systems and data. By analyzing behavior over time, UBA can detect deviations from normal activity that may indicate insider threats, compromised accounts, or policy violations. Integrating UBA with IGA allows organizations to take a more proactive approach to identity management, addressing potential issues before they escalate into security incidents.

Identity Governance and Administration is not just a technical solution; it is a critical component of an organization's overall governance, risk, and compliance (GRC) strategy. By ensuring that access to systems and data is managed securely, consistently, and in compliance with regulatory requirements, IGA helps protect organizational assets, maintain operational integrity, and build trust with customers, partners, and regulators. As the digital landscape continues to evolve, the role of IGA will become even more vital in safeguarding identities and ensuring compliance in an increasingly complex and regulated world.

Risk-Based Authentication: Adapting to Threat Levels

In the ever-evolving landscape of cybersecurity, traditional static authentication methods are increasingly inadequate to protect against sophisticated threats. Static authentication approaches, such as single-factor authentication or even basic multi-factor authentication (MFA), apply the same security measures to all users and situations, regardless of context or risk level. While these methods provide a baseline level of security, they lack the flexibility to respond to the dynamic and varied nature of modern cyber threats. This is where Risk-Based Authentication (RBA) comes into play. RBA introduces a more intelligent, adaptive approach to authentication, tailoring security measures based on the specific risk profile of each login attempt or transaction.

Risk-Based Authentication, also known as adaptive authentication, dynamically adjusts the authentication requirements based on the contextual risk of a user's behavior. Rather than treating all access attempts equally, RBA evaluates factors such as the user's location, device, login time, IP address, and behavior patterns to assess the likelihood of a threat. If an access attempt aligns with the user's normal behavior—such as logging in from a recognized device and location—the system may allow access with minimal friction, like a simple password entry. However, if the login attempt exhibits unusual characteristics, such as an unfamiliar IP address, a different geographic location, or behavior inconsistent with the user's typical patterns, the system can escalate security measures, requiring additional authentication steps such as biometric verification, one-time passwords, or even temporary account lockdowns.

The core strength of RBA lies in its ability to balance security with user convenience. One of the biggest challenges in cybersecurity is implementing strong security measures without creating a cumbersome user experience. Overly strict authentication processes can frustrate users, leading to decreased productivity, increased help desk calls, and even risky behaviors like writing down passwords or circumventing security protocols. RBA addresses this by applying stricter security only when necessary, reducing friction for legitimate users while maintaining robust defenses against suspicious activity. This adaptive approach not only enhances security but also improves user satisfaction, making it a valuable tool for organizations seeking to protect sensitive data without compromising usability.

To understand how Risk-Based Authentication works, it's essential to explore the various factors and signals used to assess risk. One of the primary factors is the user's geographic location. For example, if an employee typically logs in from an office in New York but suddenly attempts to access the system from a location in Eastern Europe, the system might flag this as a high-risk activity. The system can then respond by requiring additional verification steps or blocking the login attempt altogether. Similarly, IP address analysis can identify whether an access attempt originates from a known or trusted network or from an anonymous proxy or VPN often associated with malicious activity.

Device recognition is another critical component of RBA. By maintaining a record of trusted devices associated with a user's account, the system can quickly identify whether a login attempt comes from a familiar or unfamiliar device. If an attempt originates from a previously unseen device, especially in combination with other risk factors like an unusual location, the system can trigger additional authentication requirements. Conversely, access from a recognized device under normal conditions may allow for a streamlined login process.

Behavioral analysis plays an increasingly important role in Risk-Based Authentication. Modern RBA systems leverage machine learning algorithms to build a behavioral profile of each user based on their typical activities, such as login times, frequency, navigation patterns, and data access habits. Deviations from these established patterns can indicate potential threats. For example, if a user who typically accesses financial reports during business hours suddenly attempts to download large volumes of sensitive data late at night, the system may interpret this as suspicious behavior and require additional verification or alert security teams for further investigation.

Time-based analysis is another factor that RBA systems consider. If a user logs in at an unusual time, such as during weekends or holidays when they typically don't access the system, this can raise a red flag.

Combining this with other risk signals, such as device or location anomalies, allows the system to make a more informed decision about the level of authentication required. The use of multiple risk signals ensures a comprehensive evaluation of the context, reducing false positives while maintaining security.

One of the significant advantages of RBA is its ability to provide real-time responses to emerging threats. In traditional authentication systems, security policies are static and predefined, making it challenging to adapt to new or evolving attack vectors quickly. RBA systems, on the other hand, continuously analyze and adjust authentication requirements based on real-time data and threat intelligence. This dynamic approach allows organizations to stay ahead of attackers, responding to threats as they arise and adapting security measures to match the current risk landscape.

Risk-Based Authentication also integrates seamlessly with other security technologies and frameworks. For example, RBA can complement multi-factor authentication by determining when additional factors are necessary. Instead of applying MFA uniformly to all users and scenarios, RBA selectively enforces MFA based on risk, reducing friction for low-risk users while maintaining strong security for high-risk situations. RBA can also integrate with Security Information and Event Management (SIEM) systems to correlate authentication data with broader security events, providing a more comprehensive view of potential threats and enabling coordinated responses across the organization.

Despite its many benefits, implementing Risk-Based Authentication comes with challenges. One of the primary challenges is the complexity of accurately assessing risk without generating excessive false positives or false negatives. False positives—incorrectly identifying legitimate activities as suspicious—can lead to unnecessary authentication challenges and user frustration. False negatives—failing to identify actual threats—can result in security breaches. Striking the right balance requires careful tuning of risk assessment algorithms, continuous monitoring, and regular updates based on evolving threat landscapes and user behavior.

Another challenge is ensuring user privacy and data protection. RBA systems rely on collecting and analyzing a wide range of user data, including location, device information, and behavioral patterns. Organizations must implement robust data protection measures to ensure this information is handled securely and in compliance with privacy regulations, such as the General Data Protection Regulation (GDPR) and the California Consumer Privacy Act (CCPA). Transparency about data collection practices and providing users with control over their data are essential for maintaining trust and compliance.

The success of Risk-Based Authentication also depends on user education and awareness. Users need to understand why additional authentication steps may be required in certain situations and how these measures protect their accounts and data. Clear communication about the purpose and benefits of RBA can help reduce frustration and increase user acceptance. Additionally, organizations should provide guidance on recognizing and responding to authentication challenges, such as identifying legitimate verification requests versus phishing attempts.

As technology continues to evolve, the future of Risk-Based Authentication will be shaped by advancements in artificial intelligence (AI) and machine learning (ML). AI-driven RBA systems can analyze vast amounts of data more efficiently and accurately, improving the precision of risk assessments and reducing false positives. Machine learning algorithms can adapt to new threats and user behaviors over time, continuously refining risk models to stay ahead of attackers. These advancements will enable even more sophisticated and responsive authentication systems, enhancing security while maintaining a seamless user experience.

The rise of the Internet of Things (IoT) and the proliferation of connected devices also present new opportunities and challenges for RBA. As more devices interact with organizational systems, RBA must expand to assess the risk associated with device-based interactions. Ensuring that IoT devices are authenticated and monitored based on their behavior and context will be critical to maintaining security in increasingly complex and interconnected environments.

Risk-Based Authentication represents a significant evolution in the field of identity and access management, offering a dynamic, context-aware approach to securing digital interactions. By adapting authentication requirements to the specific risk profile of each access attempt, RBA provides a balanced solution that enhances security without compromising user experience. As cyber threats continue to grow in sophistication and complexity, organizations must embrace adaptive security measures like RBA to protect their systems and data effectively. Through continuous innovation and integration with emerging technologies, Risk-Based Authentication will play a pivotal role in the future of cybersecurity, ensuring that access to digital resources remains secure, efficient, and resilient in an ever-changing threat landscape.

The Role of Artificial Intelligence in Identity Security

As cyber threats become increasingly sophisticated and pervasive, traditional security measures often struggle to keep pace. Static rules and manual oversight are no longer sufficient to protect sensitive data and systems from evolving attack vectors. In this rapidly changing landscape, artificial intelligence (AI) has emerged as a transformative force in identity security, offering dynamic, adaptive solutions that enhance the ability to detect, prevent, and respond to threats. AI brings a new level of intelligence and automation to identity and access management (IAM), helping organizations protect their digital assets more effectively while streamlining user experiences.

Artificial intelligence plays a pivotal role in identity security by enabling systems to learn from data, recognize patterns, and make informed decisions without constant human intervention. This capability is particularly valuable in identity management, where the volume of users, devices, and transactions can overwhelm traditional security mechanisms. By analyzing vast amounts of identity-related data in real time, AI can identify anomalies, detect potential threats, and enforce security policies with unprecedented speed and accuracy.

One of the most significant contributions of AI to identity security is in the realm of anomaly detection. Traditional security systems rely on predefined rules to identify suspicious behavior, such as failed login attempts or access from unusual locations. While effective to a degree, these static rules can miss more subtle indicators of malicious activity or generate false positives that burden security teams with unnecessary alerts. AI-powered systems, on the other hand, use machine learning algorithms to establish a baseline of normal behavior for each user and continuously monitor for deviations from this baseline. For example, if an employee who typically logs in from a corporate office suddenly accesses sensitive files from a foreign country at an unusual hour, the AI system can flag this as an anomaly and trigger additional security measures.

Machine learning, a subset of AI, enhances identity security by enabling systems to adapt to new threats over time. As machine learning algorithms process more data, they become better at distinguishing between legitimate and suspicious activities. This continuous learning process allows AI-driven security systems to stay ahead of emerging threats, identifying new attack patterns and evolving tactics used by cybercriminals. For instance, AI can detect credential stuffing attacks—where attackers use stolen credentials to gain unauthorized access—by recognizing patterns of repeated login attempts from multiple IP addresses or devices, even if each attempt individually appears benign.

AI also plays a critical role in risk-based authentication (RBA), where access decisions are dynamically adjusted based on the assessed risk of each login attempt. By analyzing factors such as device type, geographic location, user behavior, and network characteristics, AI can determine the likelihood that a login attempt is legitimate or malicious. If the risk level is low, the user may be granted access with minimal friction. If the risk level is high, the system can require additional authentication factors, such as biometric verification or one-time passwords, or even block the attempt altogether. This adaptive approach balances security with user convenience, ensuring that stringent measures are applied only when necessary.

In addition to enhancing authentication processes, AI improves the efficiency and effectiveness of identity governance and administration (IGA). Managing user identities, access rights, and compliance requirements across an organization can be a complex and time-consuming task. AI simplifies these processes by automating routine tasks, such as provisioning and de-provisioning user accounts, assigning roles based on behavior patterns, and conducting access reviews. For example, AI can analyze how employees interact with systems and recommend adjustments to their access rights, ensuring that users have the appropriate permissions for their roles without accumulating unnecessary privileges. This proactive approach reduces the risk of privilege creep, where users retain access to systems they no longer need, and helps maintain compliance with regulatory standards.

AI-driven identity security also plays a crucial role in detecting and mitigating insider threats. While much attention is focused on external cyberattacks, insider threats—whether from malicious actors or unintentional mistakes—pose a significant risk to organizations. AI can monitor user behavior for signs of insider threats, such as unusual data access patterns, attempts to bypass security controls, or downloading large volumes of sensitive information. By identifying these indicators early, AI enables security teams to investigate and respond to potential threats before they result in data breaches or other security incidents.

Another key area where AI enhances identity security is in the management of biometric data. Biometric authentication methods, such as fingerprint scanning, facial recognition, and voice recognition, rely on unique physical characteristics to verify identity. AI algorithms improve the accuracy and reliability of these methods by analyzing biometric data with greater precision and adapting to variations in user behavior or environmental conditions. For example, AI can enhance facial recognition systems by accounting for changes in lighting, angles, or facial expressions, reducing the likelihood of false rejections or false acceptances. This improved accuracy not only enhances security but also makes biometric authentication more user-friendly and accessible.

AI's role in identity security extends to the broader ecosystem of cybersecurity tools and technologies. By integrating AI with security information and event management (SIEM) systems, organizations can gain a more comprehensive view of their security posture. AI can correlate identity-related data with other security events, such as network traffic anomalies or malware detections, to provide a holistic understanding of potential threats. This integrated approach enables faster, more informed decision-making and enhances the organization's ability to detect and respond to complex attacks.

The rise of AI in identity security also raises important considerations regarding privacy and ethical use of data. AI systems rely on large volumes of data to learn and make decisions, which can include sensitive personal information. Organizations must ensure that this data is collected, stored, and processed in compliance with privacy regulations, such as the General Data Protection Regulation (GDPR) and the California Consumer Privacy Act (CCPA). Transparency about how AI systems use identity data, as well as robust data protection measures, are essential to maintaining user trust and ensuring ethical practices.

Despite the many advantages of AI in identity security, it is important to recognize that AI is not a silver bullet. While AI can significantly enhance security measures, it is most effective when used in conjunction with other cybersecurity practices and technologies. Human oversight remains critical, as AI systems can sometimes produce false positives or fail to recognize novel attack techniques. Security teams must be equipped to interpret AI-generated insights, investigate alerts, and make informed decisions based on a combination of automated analysis and human expertise.

As AI technology continues to evolve, its role in identity security will likely expand, bringing new capabilities and opportunities for innovation. The development of explainable AI (XAI), which focuses on making AI decision-making processes transparent and understandable to humans, will help address concerns about the "black box" nature of AI systems. By providing clear explanations of how identity-related decisions are made, XAI can improve trust in AI-driven security measures and facilitate better collaboration between human and machine intelligence.

Another promising development is the use of AI in decentralized identity systems. Decentralized identity, which gives individuals greater control over their digital identities, can benefit from AI's ability to verify and manage credentials without relying on centralized authorities. AI can enhance the security and usability of decentralized identity solutions by automating the verification of credentials, detecting fraudulent activities, and ensuring that identity data is managed securely and efficiently across distributed networks.

The role of artificial intelligence in identity security represents a significant advancement in the way organizations protect their digital assets and manage user identities. By leveraging AI's ability to analyze data, recognize patterns, and make adaptive decisions, organizations can enhance their security posture, streamline identity management processes, and improve user experiences. As cyber threats continue to evolve and become more sophisticated, AI will remain an essential tool in the ongoing effort to safeguard identities and ensure the integrity of digital systems. Through continuous innovation, ethical practices, and integration with broader cybersecurity strategies, AI will shape the future of identity security, providing organizations with the tools they need to navigate an increasingly complex and dynamic threat landscape.

API Security and Identity Management

In the modern digital landscape, Application Programming Interfaces (APIs) have become the backbone of software development, enabling applications, services, and systems to communicate and share data seamlessly. From powering mobile apps and cloud services to integrating third-party tools and IoT devices, APIs are essential for building scalable, flexible, and interconnected solutions. However, the growing reliance on APIs has also introduced new security challenges, making API security a critical component of any organization's cybersecurity strategy. Central to securing APIs is the role of identity management, which ensures that only authorized users and systems can access sensitive data and perform specific actions.

APIs facilitate the exchange of data between different software components, often across organizational boundaries. This data can include sensitive information such as user credentials, financial transactions, and personal details. As a result, APIs are attractive targets for cybercriminals looking to exploit vulnerabilities and gain unauthorized access to systems. API security focuses on protecting these communication channels from threats such as data breaches, unauthorized access, and malicious attacks like injection, denial of service (DoS), and man-in-the-middle (MITM) attacks. Effective API security ensures that data is transmitted securely, access is properly controlled, and potential vulnerabilities are identified and mitigated.

Identity management plays a fundamental role in API security by controlling who can access APIs and what actions they can perform. Identity and Access Management (IAM) systems integrate with APIs to authenticate users and systems, authorize their actions, and ensure compliance with security policies. Authentication verifies the identity of the user or system making the API request, while authorization determines whether they have the necessary permissions to perform the requested action. Together, these processes help prevent unauthorized access and ensure that sensitive data is protected.

One of the most common methods for securing APIs is the use of tokens, particularly through standards like OAuth 2.0 and OpenID Connect. OAuth 2.0 is an authorization framework that allows applications to access resources on behalf of a user without exposing their credentials. When a user grants permission to an application, the application receives an access token that it can use to make API requests. This token-based approach provides a secure and flexible way to manage access, as tokens can be limited in scope, time-bound, and easily revoked if necessary. OpenID Connect extends OAuth 2.0 by adding an authentication layer, allowing APIs to verify the identity of users and obtain basic profile information.

API keys are another common method for authenticating API requests. An API key is a unique identifier assigned to a developer or application, which must be included in API requests to gain access. While API keys are simple to implement and use, they are less secure than token-based methods, as they do not provide fine-grained control over access permissions and can be easily compromised if exposed. To enhance security, API keys should be combined with other authentication mechanisms, such as IP whitelisting, rate limiting, and encrypted communication.

Multi-factor authentication (MFA) adds an additional layer of security to API access by requiring multiple forms of verification before granting access. For example, an API request might require both an access token and a one-time password (OTP) sent to the user's mobile device. This approach reduces the risk of unauthorized access, even if one authentication factor is compromised. MFA is particularly important for APIs that provide access to sensitive data or critical systems, where the potential impact of a security breach is significant.

Role-based access control (RBAC) and attribute-based access control (ABAC) are also important components of API security and identity management. RBAC assigns access permissions based on predefined roles, such as "admin," "user," or "guest," ensuring that users can only perform actions appropriate to their role. ABAC, on the other hand, uses a more dynamic approach, evaluating attributes such as user identity, resource type, and environmental conditions to determine access rights. By integrating RBAC and ABAC with API security, organizations can enforce granular access controls that align with their security policies and business requirements.

Encryption is a critical element of API security, ensuring that data transmitted between clients and servers is protected from interception and tampering. Transport Layer Security (TLS) is the standard protocol for securing API communication, providing end-to-end encryption and data integrity. APIs should enforce the use of HTTPS, which leverages TLS to encrypt data in transit, preventing attackers from eavesdropping or modifying the data. Additionally, sensitive data within API payloads should be encrypted at rest, ensuring that it remains secure even if the underlying storage systems are compromised.

Rate limiting and throttling are important techniques for protecting APIs from abuse and denial-of-service attacks. By limiting the number of API requests that can be made within a specific time frame, organizations can prevent malicious actors from overwhelming their systems and ensure that resources are available for legitimate users. Rate limiting can be applied at various levels, such as per user, per IP address, or per API key, providing flexible control over API usage. Throttling goes a step further by dynamically adjusting the rate limits based on system load and user behavior, ensuring optimal performance and security.

Monitoring and logging are essential for detecting and responding to API security incidents. API gateways and management platforms provide tools for tracking API usage, identifying anomalies, and generating alerts for suspicious activity. Logs should capture detailed information about API requests, including timestamps, user identities, request parameters, and response codes. This data is invaluable for forensic analysis, helping organizations investigate security breaches, identify vulnerabilities, and improve their API security posture. Integrating API logs with Security Information and Event Management (SIEM) systems enables real-time monitoring and correlation with other security events, providing a comprehensive view of potential threats.

The use of artificial intelligence (AI) and machine learning (ML) is transforming API security and identity management by enabling more sophisticated threat detection and response. AI-driven systems can analyze large volumes of API traffic to identify patterns and detect anomalies that may indicate malicious activity. For example, machine learning algorithms can recognize unusual login attempts, unexpected data access patterns, or spikes in API requests that deviate from normal behavior. By continuously learning from data, these systems can adapt to new threats and provide proactive protection against emerging attack vectors.

As organizations increasingly adopt microservices architectures and cloud-native applications, securing APIs becomes even more complex. In a microservices environment, APIs are used extensively to enable communication between services, each with its own set of access controls and security requirements. API security in this context requires a consistent and scalable approach to identity management, ensuring that authentication and authorization mechanisms are applied uniformly across all services. API gateways play a crucial role in this process, acting as intermediaries that enforce security policies, manage access tokens, and monitor API traffic.

The integration of APIs with third-party services and partners introduces additional security considerations. Organizations must ensure that external APIs are properly vetted, secured, and monitored to prevent unauthorized access and data breaches. This includes implementing strong authentication mechanisms, such as OAuth and mutual TLS, and establishing clear contracts and service-level agreements (SLAs) that define security expectations and responsibilities. Regular security assessments and audits of third-party APIs help identify vulnerabilities and ensure compliance with security standards.

Compliance with regulatory requirements is another important aspect of API security and identity management. Regulations such as the General Data Protection Regulation (GDPR), the Health Insurance Portability and Accountability Act (HIPAA), and the Payment Card Industry Data Security Standard (PCI DSS) impose strict requirements on how data is accessed, transmitted, and stored. API security measures must align with these regulations, ensuring that sensitive data is protected and that access controls are enforced consistently. Organizations should implement comprehensive data protection policies, conduct regular compliance audits, and maintain detailed records of API access and usage to demonstrate compliance.

The role of API security and identity management is critical in safeguarding the integrity, confidentiality, and availability of digital systems. As APIs continue to drive innovation and connectivity, organizations must prioritize robust security measures to protect against evolving threats and ensure secure access to their resources. By integrating advanced authentication mechanisms, enforcing granular access controls, and leveraging AI-driven threat detection, organizations can build a resilient API security framework that supports their business objectives while protecting sensitive data and systems. As technology continues to evolve, the principles of API security and identity management will remain essential to navigating the challenges and opportunities of the digital age.

Securing Mobile Authentication: Challenges and Solutions

As mobile devices have become integral to both personal and professional lives, securing mobile authentication has emerged as a critical component of cybersecurity. With smartphones and tablets providing access to sensitive information, financial data, corporate systems, and personal communications, the security of mobile authentication directly impacts data protection and user privacy. The convenience and ubiquity of mobile technology have revolutionized how we interact with digital services, but they have also introduced a new set of challenges and vulnerabilities that must be addressed to ensure secure access.

One of the primary challenges in securing mobile authentication is the diverse and fragmented nature of the mobile ecosystem. Unlike desktop environments, which are typically more standardized, mobile platforms encompass a wide range of operating systems, devices, manufacturers, and app stores. Each of these elements introduces unique security considerations, making it difficult to implement a one-size-fits-all approach to mobile authentication. For example, Android devices, with their open-source nature and varying levels of manufacturer control, present different security challenges compared to the more tightly controlled iOS ecosystem. Ensuring consistent security across such a heterogeneous landscape requires flexible, adaptable authentication solutions.

Mobile devices are also inherently more exposed to physical threats than traditional computers. The portability that makes smartphones so convenient also increases the risk of loss or theft. When a mobile device falls into the wrong hands, any stored credentials, saved passwords, or automatically logged-in apps become potential entry points for unauthorized access. While device encryption and remote wipe capabilities can mitigate some of this risk, ensuring robust authentication methods that prevent unauthorized access even if a device is compromised remains essential.

The reliance on passwords for mobile authentication presents another significant challenge. Passwords are notoriously vulnerable to a range of attacks, including phishing, brute force, and credential stuffing. On mobile devices, the difficulty of typing complex passwords on small touchscreens often leads users to choose weak, easily guessable passwords or to reuse passwords across multiple accounts. This behavior increases the risk of account compromise, particularly as attackers increasingly target mobile platforms with sophisticated phishing schemes designed to exploit these weaknesses.

Biometric authentication has become a popular alternative to traditional passwords on mobile devices, leveraging unique physical characteristics such as fingerprints, facial recognition, and iris scans.

While biometrics offer enhanced security and convenience, they are not without their challenges. Biometric data, unlike passwords, cannot be changed if compromised. If an attacker successfully spoofs a fingerprint or facial recognition system—or if biometric data is stolen from a device or server—the affected user may be permanently at risk. Additionally, biometric systems can sometimes be bypassed with physical artifacts, such as high-resolution photos or 3D-printed models, particularly on devices with less sophisticated sensors.

Another challenge in securing mobile authentication is the prevalence of insecure app development practices. Many mobile applications fail to implement robust security measures, such as secure communication protocols, proper session management, and strong encryption. Inadequate security in app development can lead to vulnerabilities that attackers can exploit to bypass authentication mechanisms or intercept sensitive data. Furthermore, the use of third-party libraries and frameworks in app development can introduce additional risks if these components contain security flaws.

The use of mobile devices on public or unsecured networks adds another layer of complexity to mobile authentication security. Public Wi-Fi networks, commonly found in cafes, airports, and hotels, are prime targets for attackers seeking to intercept data transmissions and compromise user credentials. Without proper encryption and secure communication protocols, authentication data transmitted over these networks can be easily captured and exploited. Even on secure networks, mobile devices are susceptible to man-in-the-middle (MITM) attacks, where an attacker intercepts and potentially alters communication between the device and the authentication server.

To address these challenges, a multi-layered approach to mobile authentication security is essential. One of the most effective strategies is the adoption of multi-factor authentication (MFA), which requires users to provide multiple forms of verification before gaining access. MFA can combine something the user knows (a password or PIN), something the user has (a mobile device or security token), and something the user is (biometric data). By layering these factors, MFA significantly reduces the risk of unauthorized access, even if one authentication method is compromised.

Implementing strong biometric authentication systems is another key solution. To enhance the security of biometric data, devices should use secure enclaves or trusted execution environments (TEEs) to store and process biometric information. These secure areas of the device's hardware are isolated from the main operating system, protecting biometric data from tampering or unauthorized access. Additionally, biometric systems should employ liveness detection techniques to differentiate between real users and spoofed artifacts, such as photos or fake fingerprints. Regular updates and improvements to biometric algorithms are also essential to stay ahead of emerging spoofing techniques.

Encryption plays a vital role in securing mobile authentication. Data transmitted between mobile devices and authentication servers should always be encrypted using strong protocols such as Transport Layer Security (TLS). This ensures that authentication credentials and other sensitive information are protected from interception during transmission. On the device itself, sensitive data should be encrypted at rest, using robust encryption algorithms to prevent unauthorized access if the device is lost or stolen. Ensuring that encryption keys are securely managed and stored is also critical to maintaining the integrity of encrypted data.

Secure app development practices are fundamental to mobile authentication security. Developers should follow established security guidelines, such as those provided by the Open Web Application Security Project (OWASP) Mobile Security Project, to build secure mobile applications. This includes implementing secure coding practices, performing regular security testing and code reviews, and using secure libraries and frameworks. Proper session management is also essential, ensuring that authentication tokens are securely stored, transmitted, and invalidated when no longer needed. Developers should avoid storing sensitive information, such as passwords or authentication tokens, in plaintext or in insecure storage locations.

Educating users about mobile security best practices is another important aspect of securing mobile authentication. Users should be encouraged to create strong, unique passwords and to enable multi-factor authentication wherever possible. They should also be aware of the risks associated with public Wi-Fi networks and advised to use virtual private networks (VPNs) to encrypt their data when accessing sensitive information over unsecured connections. Regular security updates and patches should be applied to mobile devices and applications to protect against known vulnerabilities.

The use of device attestation and trust frameworks can further enhance mobile authentication security. Device attestation verifies the integrity of the device and its environment before granting access, ensuring that the device has not been compromised or tampered with. Trust frameworks can assess the risk associated with a device or user based on factors such as device health, location, and behavior patterns. By incorporating these assessments into the authentication process, organizations can dynamically adjust security measures based on the risk level, providing stronger protection against potential threats.

As mobile technology continues to evolve, the role of artificial intelligence (AI) and machine learning (ML) in securing mobile authentication is becoming increasingly significant. AI and ML can analyze user behavior and device interactions to detect anomalies and potential security threats. For example, if a user typically logs in from the same geographic location and suddenly attempts to authenticate from a different country, the system can flag this behavior and require additional verification. By continuously learning from data, AI-driven systems can adapt to new threats and provide proactive protection against emerging risks.

The integration of mobile authentication with broader identity and access management (IAM) frameworks is also crucial for maintaining consistent security across an organization's digital ecosystem. By centralizing identity management and applying uniform security policies, organizations can ensure that mobile authentication aligns with their overall cybersecurity strategy. Single sign-on (SSO) solutions can streamline the authentication process for mobile users, allowing them to access multiple applications and services with a single set of credentials while maintaining strong security controls.

In conclusion, securing mobile authentication is a multifaceted challenge that requires a combination of advanced technologies, secure development practices, user education, and continuous monitoring. By adopting a holistic approach that incorporates multi-factor authentication, biometric security, encryption, and AI-driven threat detection, organizations can protect their mobile ecosystems from a wide range of threats. As mobile devices continue to play an increasingly central role in our digital lives, ensuring the security of mobile authentication will remain a critical priority for individuals and organizations alike.

The Human Factor: User Behavior and Identity Security

In the realm of cybersecurity, technology is often viewed as the frontline defense against threats. Firewalls, encryption, multi-factor authentication, and other technological solutions are designed to safeguard data and systems. However, even the most sophisticated security infrastructure can be compromised by a single weak link: human behavior. The human factor remains one of the most significant challenges in identity security, as user actions, whether intentional or accidental, often open doors to security breaches. Understanding how user behavior impacts identity security is critical to developing effective strategies for protecting sensitive information and systems.

Human error is frequently cited as a leading cause of security breaches. Despite continuous advancements in security technology, users often fall prey to common mistakes such as using weak passwords, reusing credentials across multiple platforms, and falling for phishing scams. These behaviors create vulnerabilities that attackers are quick to exploit. For instance, a user who uses the same simple password for both personal and professional accounts inadvertently exposes their organization to risk if one of those accounts is compromised. Password reuse becomes particularly dangerous when data breaches from one service lead to credential stuffing attacks on others, where hackers attempt to use stolen credentials across various platforms.

Phishing remains one of the most effective methods for attackers to compromise identity security. These social engineering attacks rely on deceiving users into revealing sensitive information, such as login credentials or personal data, by posing as legitimate entities. Phishing emails often mimic trusted organizations, using convincing language and visual cues to lure users into clicking malicious links or downloading harmful attachments. Despite widespread awareness of phishing tactics, many users still fall victim due to the increasing sophistication of these schemes. Spear-phishing, a targeted form of phishing that focuses on specific individuals or organizations, is particularly dangerous as it leverages personalized information to increase credibility and success rates.

Another common user behavior that compromises identity security is the mishandling of sensitive data. Users often underestimate the importance of protecting personal and organizational information. For example, sharing login credentials with colleagues, writing down passwords, or leaving devices unattended in public places can all lead to unauthorized access. Even seemingly harmless actions, such as discussing work-related topics on social media or using unsecured public Wi-Fi networks, can provide attackers with valuable information for launching targeted attacks.

The rise of remote work and bring-your-own-device (BYOD) policies has further complicated identity security. While these practices offer flexibility and convenience, they also blur the lines between personal and professional device use, increasing the risk of data breaches. Users accessing corporate systems from personal devices or unsecured networks expose their organizations to potential threats. Furthermore, the lack of consistent security measures across different devices and environments makes it challenging to enforce identity security policies effectively.

Addressing the human factor in identity security requires a multifaceted approach that combines technology, education, and organizational culture. One of the most effective strategies is to implement robust user education and awareness programs. Training users to recognize phishing attempts, create strong passwords, and follow best practices for handling sensitive data is essential. Regular security awareness training can help reinforce these principles, keeping users informed about the latest threats and how to avoid them. Simulated phishing exercises, where users are tested with mock phishing emails, can be particularly effective in raising awareness and identifying individuals who may need additional training.

Creating a culture of security within an organization is equally important. When security is ingrained in the organizational culture, users are more likely to adopt secure behaviors and take responsibility for protecting sensitive information. Leadership plays a crucial role in setting the tone for this culture by prioritizing security initiatives, promoting transparency, and encouraging open communication about security concerns. Recognizing and rewarding secure behavior can also motivate users to adhere to best practices.

While education and culture are vital, technological solutions remain an essential component of mitigating the human factor in identity security. Multi-factor authentication (MFA) is one of the most effective tools for reducing the risk associated with compromised credentials. By requiring multiple forms of verification—such as a password, a fingerprint, or a one-time code sent to a mobile device—MFA adds an additional layer of security that makes it significantly more difficult for attackers to gain unauthorized access, even if they obtain a user's password.

Password management tools can also help users adopt more secure behaviors. These tools generate and store complex, unique passwords for each account, reducing the likelihood of password reuse and simplifying the process of managing multiple credentials. By automating password management, users are less likely to resort to insecure practices such as writing down passwords or using easily guessable phrases.

Behavioral analytics and machine learning are increasingly being used to enhance identity security by monitoring user behavior for anomalies. These systems establish a baseline of normal activity for each user and flag deviations that may indicate a security threat. For example, if a user typically logs in from the same location and suddenly accesses the system from a different country, the system can trigger an alert or require additional authentication. Similarly, if a user who usually accesses a limited set of files begins downloading large volumes of sensitive data, the system can intervene to prevent potential data exfiltration. By continuously analyzing user behavior, these technologies provide real-time insights and responses to potential threats.

Despite the availability of advanced technologies and training programs, overcoming the human factor in identity security remains a persistent challenge. Users are often the last line of defense against cyber threats, and their actions can have far-reaching consequences. Organizations must recognize that identity security is not solely a technological issue but a human one as well. By addressing the behaviors and attitudes that contribute to security vulnerabilities, organizations can create a more resilient and secure environment.

One emerging trend in addressing the human factor is the use of gamification and interactive learning techniques to engage users in security training. By incorporating elements of competition, rewards, and real-world scenarios, these approaches make learning about security more engaging and memorable. For example, security awareness games that simulate phishing attacks or data breaches can help users understand the impact of their actions in a safe and controlled environment. This hands-on experience reinforces the importance of secure behavior and helps users retain critical information.

Another important consideration is the role of user-centric design in identity security solutions. Systems that are difficult to use or overly complex can frustrate users and lead to insecure workarounds. For example, if a password policy requires frequent changes and overly complex combinations, users may resort to writing down passwords or using predictable patterns. Designing security solutions with the user in mind—emphasizing ease of use, accessibility, and minimal disruption—can encourage compliance and reduce the likelihood of risky behavior. Single sign-on (SSO) solutions, which allow users to access multiple applications with a single set of credentials, are an example of user-centric design that enhances security while simplifying the login process.

Ultimately, addressing the human factor in identity security requires a holistic approach that integrates education, culture, technology, and design. By understanding the motivations and behaviors that lead to security vulnerabilities, organizations can develop strategies that not only protect against threats but also empower users to become active participants in maintaining security. As the digital landscape continues to evolve, the importance of addressing the human element in identity security will remain paramount. By fostering a culture of awareness, leveraging advanced technologies, and prioritizing user-friendly solutions, organizations can build a robust defense against the ever-present risks posed by human behavior in the digital world.

Cloud Identity Management: Navigating the New Normal

As organizations increasingly migrate their operations to the cloud, identity management has become a cornerstone of modern cybersecurity strategies. The shift to cloud computing offers unparalleled flexibility, scalability, and efficiency, but it also introduces new complexities and risks related to managing digital identities. Cloud Identity Management (CIM) has emerged as a critical solution to navigate this new normal, providing the tools and frameworks necessary to secure access to cloud resources while maintaining operational agility. Understanding the challenges and opportunities of cloud identity management is essential for organizations looking to protect their assets in an increasingly interconnected digital landscape.

In traditional IT environments, identity management was largely confined within the boundaries of an organization's on-premises infrastructure. Centralized directories, such as Microsoft Active Directory, were used to manage user identities and control access to internal resources. However, the transition to cloud services has fundamentally altered this paradigm. With applications, data, and services distributed across multiple cloud providers and platforms, the traditional perimeter-based security model is no longer sufficient. Instead, identity has become the new perimeter, and managing it effectively in the cloud requires a rethinking of traditional approaches.

One of the primary challenges of cloud identity management is the need to handle a diverse and dynamic range of users, devices, and services. Employees, contractors, partners, and customers all require access to cloud resources, often from various locations and devices. This complexity is further compounded by the proliferation of Software-as-a-Service (SaaS) applications, each with its own identity management requirements. Without a unified approach, managing identities across multiple platforms can lead to inconsistent security policies, increased administrative overhead, and a higher risk of security breaches.

Cloud Identity and Access Management (CIAM) solutions address these challenges by providing centralized control over user identities and access rights across cloud environments. These solutions enable organizations to manage who has access to what resources, enforce security policies, and ensure compliance with regulatory requirements. By integrating with cloud service providers, CIAM platforms offer seamless access to cloud applications while maintaining robust security controls. This centralized approach simplifies identity management, reduces administrative burdens, and enhances security by ensuring consistent enforcement of access policies.

One of the key features of cloud identity management is Single Sign-On (SSO), which allows users to authenticate once and gain access to multiple applications and services without needing to log in separately to each one. SSO enhances user convenience and productivity by reducing the need to remember multiple passwords while also improving security by minimizing the attack surface associated with credential management. By leveraging federated identity protocols, such as SAML (Security Assertion Markup Language) and OpenID Connect, SSO enables secure authentication across different domains and platforms, facilitating seamless access to both on-premises and cloud resources.

Multi-Factor Authentication (MFA) is another critical component of cloud identity management, providing an additional layer of security beyond traditional username and password authentication. MFA requires users to provide multiple forms of verification, such as a password and a one-time code sent to their mobile device or a biometric factor like a fingerprint or facial recognition. By requiring multiple authentication factors, MFA significantly reduces the risk of unauthorized access, even if one credential is compromised. In the context of cloud identity management, MFA is essential for protecting sensitive data and applications from increasingly sophisticated cyber threats.

Role-Based Access Control (RBAC) and Attribute-Based Access Control (ABAC) are essential mechanisms for managing access in cloud environments. RBAC assigns permissions based on predefined roles within the organization, ensuring that users have access only to the resources necessary for their job functions. ABAC, on the other hand, provides more granular control by evaluating attributes such as user identity, resource type, and environmental context to determine access rights. By implementing RBAC and ABAC in cloud identity management, organizations can enforce the principle of least privilege, reducing the risk of over-permissioning and minimizing potential attack vectors.

The integration of identity governance into cloud identity management is crucial for ensuring compliance with regulatory requirements and maintaining security. Identity Governance and Administration (IGA) tools provide capabilities for managing the entire lifecycle of user identities, from onboarding and role assignment to access reviews and de-provisioning. Automated workflows streamline the process of granting and revoking access, ensuring that permissions are aligned with organizational policies and that orphaned accounts are promptly deactivated. Regular access reviews and audits help identify and mitigate risks associated with excessive or inappropriate access, supporting compliance with regulations such as GDPR, HIPAA, and SOX.

Cloud identity management also plays a vital role in supporting Zero Trust Architecture (ZTA), a security model that assumes no user or device can be trusted by default, regardless of their location within or outside the network. In a Zero Trust environment, identity verification is continuous, and access decisions are based on real-time assessments of risk. Cloud identity management solutions enable organizations to implement Zero Trust principles by providing robust authentication, granular access controls, and continuous monitoring of user activity. By integrating with security information and event management (SIEM) systems, cloud identity platforms can detect anomalies and respond to potential threats in real time, enhancing overall security posture.

As organizations increasingly adopt hybrid and multi-cloud environments, cloud identity management must support interoperability across different platforms and providers. This requires the use of standardized protocols and APIs that enable seamless integration and consistent policy enforcement across diverse environments. Cloud identity federation allows organizations to extend their identity management capabilities to external partners and services, facilitating secure collaboration while maintaining control over access. By adopting a federated identity approach, organizations can streamline user access, reduce administrative complexity, and enhance security across their entire digital ecosystem.

The rise of decentralized identity solutions represents a promising development in cloud identity management. Decentralized identity frameworks, such as those based on blockchain technology, empower individuals to own and control their digital identities without relying on centralized authorities. By using cryptographic proofs and verifiable credentials, decentralized identity systems provide secure and privacy-respecting authentication mechanisms that can be integrated into cloud environments. This approach enhances user privacy, reduces the risk of identity theft, and supports compliance with data protection regulations.

Artificial intelligence (AI) and machine learning (ML) are also transforming cloud identity management by enabling more sophisticated threat detection and response capabilities. AI-driven identity analytics can analyze user behavior, detect anomalies, and identify potential security risks in real time. For example, if a user who typically accesses cloud resources during business hours suddenly logs in from an unfamiliar location at an unusual time, the system can flag this behavior for further investigation or trigger additional authentication requirements. Machine learning algorithms continuously refine their models based on new data, improving the accuracy and effectiveness of identity security measures over time.

Despite the many benefits of cloud identity management, organizations must remain vigilant about potential risks and challenges. Misconfigurations, such as improperly set access controls or exposed APIs, can create vulnerabilities that attackers can exploit. Ensuring that cloud identity management solutions are properly configured, regularly updated, and continuously monitored is essential for maintaining security. Additionally, organizations must balance the need for robust security with the user experience, ensuring that authentication processes are secure without being overly cumbersome.

Cloud identity management is an essential element of modern cybersecurity, enabling organizations to navigate the complexities of the cloud while protecting sensitive data and resources. By adopting comprehensive identity management strategies that incorporate SSO, MFA, RBAC, ABAC, and identity governance, organizations can enhance security, streamline operations, and ensure compliance with regulatory requirements. As cloud technologies continue to evolve, the role of cloud identity management will become increasingly critical in safeguarding digital identities and maintaining trust in an interconnected world. By embracing innovative solutions, such as decentralized identity frameworks and AI-driven analytics, organizations can stay ahead of emerging threats and build a resilient security foundation for the future.

Identity as a Service (IDaaS): The Rise of Cloud Solutions

The rapid evolution of cloud technology has transformed the way organizations manage their IT infrastructure, data, and applications. Among the many services that have migrated to the cloud, identity management has emerged as a critical area of focus. Identity as a Service (IDaaS) represents a significant shift in how organizations handle identity and access management (IAM), providing scalable, cloud-based solutions that enhance security, streamline operations, and support digital transformation initiatives. As businesses continue to adopt cloud-first strategies, IDaaS has become an essential component of modern cybersecurity frameworks.

Identity as a Service refers to the delivery of identity and access management capabilities through the cloud. Rather than relying on traditional, on-premises IAM systems, organizations can leverage IDaaS platforms to manage user identities, authenticate access, and enforce security policies across diverse environments. These platforms offer a range of features, including Single Sign-On (SSO), Multi-Factor Authentication (MFA), directory services, identity governance, and access provisioning, all delivered as a cloud-based service. By outsourcing identity management to specialized providers, organizations can benefit from enhanced security, reduced operational complexity, and greater flexibility in managing digital identities.

One of the primary drivers behind the rise of IDaaS is the growing complexity of managing identities in today's digital landscape. Organizations now operate in hybrid environments that span on-premises systems, cloud applications, mobile devices, and remote workforces. This complexity makes it challenging to maintain consistent security policies and manage access across multiple platforms. IDaaS addresses these challenges by providing a centralized, cloud-based solution that integrates with a wide range of applications and services, ensuring seamless and secure access for users regardless of their location or device.

Single Sign-On is a key feature of IDaaS platforms, allowing users to authenticate once and gain access to multiple applications without needing to log in separately to each one. This not only enhances user convenience and productivity but also reduces the risk associated with password fatigue and credential reuse. By minimizing the number of passwords users need to remember and manage, SSO helps prevent common security issues such as weak passwords and phishing attacks. IDaaS platforms use federated identity protocols, such as SAML (Security Assertion Markup Language) and OpenID Connect, to enable secure and interoperable authentication across different domains and applications.

Multi-Factor Authentication is another critical component of IDaaS, providing an additional layer of security beyond traditional username and password authentication. MFA requires users to verify their identity using multiple factors, such as something they know (a password), something they have (a mobile device or security token), and something they are (biometric data like a fingerprint or facial recognition). By incorporating MFA into the authentication process, IDaaS platforms significantly reduce the risk of unauthorized access, even if a user's credentials are compromised. This is particularly important in protecting sensitive data and applications from increasingly sophisticated cyber threats.

IDaaS platforms also offer robust directory services, enabling organizations to manage user identities and attributes in a centralized, cloud-based directory. These directories can synchronize with existing on-premises directories, such as Microsoft Active Directory or LDAP (Lightweight Directory Access Protocol), ensuring that identity information is consistent and up-to-date across all systems. This integration simplifies identity management in hybrid environments and supports seamless user provisioning and de-provisioning. Automated provisioning ensures that new employees are granted the appropriate access rights from day one, while automated de-provisioning ensures that access is promptly revoked when employees leave the organization, reducing the risk of orphaned accounts and unauthorized access.

Identity governance is a crucial aspect of IDaaS, providing organizations with the tools to enforce access policies, conduct access reviews, and ensure compliance with regulatory requirements. IDaaS platforms offer features such as role-based access control (RBAC), attribute-based access control (ABAC), and segregation of duties (SoD) to manage and monitor access to resources. These capabilities help organizations enforce the principle of least privilege, ensuring that users have access only to the resources necessary for their job functions. Regular access reviews and audit logs provide visibility into user activities, supporting compliance with regulations such as GDPR, HIPAA, and SOX.

The scalability and flexibility of IDaaS make it an attractive solution for organizations of all sizes. Unlike traditional IAM systems, which often require significant upfront investment in hardware, software, and maintenance, IDaaS platforms operate on a subscription-based model, allowing organizations to pay for only the services they need. This model provides predictable costs and eliminates the need for ongoing infrastructure management, freeing up IT resources to focus on strategic initiatives. Additionally, IDaaS platforms can easily scale to accommodate growing user bases, new applications, and evolving security requirements, making them well-suited for dynamic business environments.

Another advantage of IDaaS is its ability to support remote work and mobile access. As the workforce becomes increasingly distributed, employees need secure access to corporate resources from various locations and devices. IDaaS platforms provide secure, cloud-based authentication and access management, enabling users to connect to applications and data from anywhere in the world. This capability is essential for supporting remote work, enabling business continuity, and enhancing productivity in today's flexible work environments.

While IDaaS offers numerous benefits, it also presents certain challenges and considerations. One of the primary concerns is data security and privacy. By outsourcing identity management to a third-party provider, organizations must ensure that their data is protected and that the provider adheres to stringent security standards. This includes implementing robust encryption for data at rest and in transit, conducting regular security audits, and ensuring compliance with relevant data protection regulations. Organizations should also evaluate the provider's incident response capabilities and ensure that they have clear protocols in place for handling security breaches.

Integration with existing systems and applications can also be a challenge when adopting IDaaS. Organizations with complex IT environments may face difficulties in ensuring seamless interoperability between the IDaaS platform and their legacy systems. To address this, IDaaS providers offer a range of integration tools, APIs, and connectors to facilitate the integration process. It is essential for organizations to conduct thorough planning and testing to ensure that the IDaaS solution integrates smoothly with their existing infrastructure and meets their specific business requirements.

Another important consideration is the potential for vendor lock-in. Relying on a single IDaaS provider for identity management can create dependencies that may limit flexibility in the future. To mitigate this risk, organizations should choose IDaaS platforms that support open standards and interoperability, allowing them to switch providers or integrate with other solutions as needed. Additionally, organizations should have clear exit strategies and data migration plans in place to ensure that they can transition smoothly if they decide to change providers.

The rise of IDaaS is closely linked to broader trends in digital transformation and cloud adoption. As organizations continue to embrace cloud technologies, the need for secure, scalable, and flexible identity management solutions will only grow. IDaaS platforms provide the foundation for secure digital interactions, enabling organizations to protect their assets, comply with regulatory requirements, and deliver seamless user experiences. By leveraging the capabilities of IDaaS, organizations can enhance their cybersecurity posture, improve operational efficiency, and support innovation in an increasingly connected world.

Emerging technologies, such as artificial intelligence (AI) and machine learning (ML), are further enhancing the capabilities of IDaaS platforms. AI-driven identity analytics can detect anomalies, predict potential security threats, and automate identity-related tasks, such as access provisioning and compliance reporting. Machine learning algorithms continuously refine their models based on new data, improving the accuracy and effectiveness of identity security measures over time. These advancements enable organizations to stay ahead of evolving threats and ensure that their identity management practices remain robust and adaptive.

As the digital landscape continues to evolve, Identity as a Service will play an increasingly vital role in helping organizations navigate the complexities of identity management in the cloud. By embracing IDaaS solutions, organizations can build a resilient, secure, and agile identity management framework that supports their strategic goals and drives success in the digital age. Through continuous innovation and a commitment to best practices, IDaaS will remain at the forefront of cybersecurity, enabling organizations to protect their digital identities and thrive in an ever-changing technological environment.

Challenges of Identity Management in Hybrid Environments

As organizations increasingly adopt hybrid environments—combining on-premises infrastructure with cloud-based services—managing identities and access has become more complex than ever before. Hybrid environments offer businesses the flexibility to leverage the scalability and cost-efficiency of cloud solutions while maintaining control over sensitive data and legacy systems within their own data centers. However, this blend of traditional and modern infrastructures introduces unique challenges in ensuring secure, consistent, and efficient identity management. Navigating these challenges requires organizations to rethink their identity and access management (IAM) strategies, balancing the demands of security, compliance, and user experience across diverse platforms.

One of the primary challenges in hybrid identity management is maintaining a unified identity across both on-premises and cloud environments. Traditionally, organizations relied on centralized directories like Microsoft Active Directory (AD) to manage user identities within their corporate networks. However, as businesses adopt Software-as-a-Service (SaaS) applications and cloud platforms such as Microsoft Azure, Amazon Web Services (AWS), and Google Cloud, they must extend their identity management capabilities beyond the confines of their local infrastructure. Ensuring that user identities are synchronized and consistent across both environments is critical to maintaining security and providing seamless access to resources.

Identity synchronization between on-premises directories and cloud-based identity providers can be technically challenging. Organizations often use directory synchronization tools, such as Azure AD Connect, to bridge the gap between their local Active Directory and Azure Active Directory. While these tools help maintain consistency, they also introduce complexities related to data replication, latency, and conflict resolution. For example, discrepancies between on-premises and cloud directories can lead to issues with user authentication, access rights, and group memberships. Addressing these issues requires careful configuration and ongoing management to ensure that identity data remains accurate and up-to-date across all systems.

Another significant challenge is managing access controls consistently across hybrid environments. On-premises systems and cloud platforms often have different access control models, policies, and mechanisms. For instance, legacy applications may rely on traditional role-based access control (RBAC) mechanisms, while modern cloud applications might use attribute-based access control (ABAC) or even policy-based access control (PBAC). Harmonizing these diverse access control models to enforce consistent security policies can be difficult, especially when dealing with a wide range of applications, services, and user roles. Organizations must develop comprehensive access management strategies that account for the unique requirements of both their on-premises and cloud environments.

Security is a paramount concern in hybrid identity management. The expansion of an organization's IT footprint to the cloud increases the attack surface, exposing new vulnerabilities that must be addressed. Hybrid environments are particularly susceptible to identity-based attacks, such as credential stuffing, phishing, and man-in-the-middle attacks. Ensuring secure authentication and authorization processes across both environments is essential to mitigating these risks. Multi-Factor Authentication (MFA) is a critical tool in this regard, adding an additional layer of security by requiring users to verify their identities using multiple factors, such as a password, a mobile device, or biometric data.

However, implementing MFA consistently across hybrid environments can be challenging. On-premises systems may not natively support modern MFA methods, requiring additional integration and customization efforts. Moreover, ensuring a seamless user experience while enforcing strong security measures can be difficult, as users may become frustrated with inconsistent authentication processes or excessive security prompts. Striking the right balance between security and usability is crucial to the success of hybrid identity management initiatives.

Another security challenge is managing privileged access in hybrid environments. Privileged accounts, such as system administrators and IT managers, have elevated access rights that allow them to control critical infrastructure and sensitive data. In a hybrid environment, these accounts often span both on-premises and cloud systems, increasing the complexity of managing and monitoring their activities. Privileged Access Management (PAM) solutions are essential for securing these accounts, providing tools for enforcing least privilege access, monitoring privileged activities, and detecting potential security threats. Integrating PAM solutions across hybrid environments requires careful planning and coordination to ensure consistent enforcement of security policies.

Compliance with regulatory requirements is another significant challenge in hybrid identity management. Organizations operating in regulated industries, such as finance, healthcare, and government, must adhere to strict data protection and privacy regulations, including GDPR, HIPAA, and SOX. Ensuring compliance across both on-premises and cloud environments requires comprehensive identity governance and auditing capabilities. Organizations must implement processes for tracking user access, conducting regular access reviews, and generating detailed audit logs to demonstrate compliance with regulatory standards.

However, achieving consistent compliance in hybrid environments can be difficult due to differences in data handling practices, security controls, and auditing capabilities between on-premises and cloud platforms. For example, cloud service providers may offer built-in compliance tools and certifications, but these tools may not align perfectly with an organization's on-premises compliance requirements. Bridging this gap requires organizations to develop integrated compliance strategies that account for the unique characteristics of both environments.

The complexity of hybrid environments also introduces challenges related to user lifecycle management. Managing the entire lifecycle of user identities—from onboarding and role assignment to access provisioning and de-provisioning—becomes more complicated when dealing with multiple platforms and systems. Automated identity lifecycle management tools can help streamline these processes, ensuring that user access rights are granted and revoked promptly and accurately. However, integrating these tools across hybrid environments requires careful coordination to avoid inconsistencies and ensure that identity data remains synchronized.

User experience is another critical consideration in hybrid identity management. Users expect seamless access to applications and resources, regardless of whether they are hosted on-premises or in the cloud. Inconsistent authentication processes, access delays, and fragmented user interfaces can lead to frustration and decreased productivity. Single Sign-On (SSO) solutions are essential for providing a unified user experience, allowing users to authenticate once and gain access to multiple applications across both environments. Implementing SSO in hybrid environments requires integrating diverse authentication protocols and ensuring interoperability between on-premises and cloud systems.

The role of artificial intelligence (AI) and machine learning (ML) in hybrid identity management is growing, offering new opportunities to enhance security and streamline operations. AI-driven identity analytics can detect anomalies in user behavior, identify potential security threats, and automate identity management tasks. For example, machine learning algorithms can analyze login patterns to detect unusual access attempts, such as a user logging in from an unfamiliar location or device. By continuously learning from data, these systems can adapt to evolving threats and provide proactive protection against identity-related risks.

Despite the challenges, hybrid environments also offer opportunities to leverage the strengths of both on-premises and cloud systems. Organizations can take advantage of the scalability and flexibility of cloud services while maintaining control over sensitive data and legacy systems within their own data centers. By adopting a comprehensive and integrated approach to identity management, organizations can navigate the complexities of hybrid environments and achieve a balance between security, compliance, and user experience.

Developing a successful hybrid identity management strategy requires a clear understanding of the organization's IT landscape, security requirements, and business objectives. Organizations must invest in the right tools, technologies, and processes to ensure that identities are managed consistently and securely across all platforms. This includes implementing robust identity governance frameworks, integrating IAM and PAM solutions, and leveraging AI-driven analytics to enhance security and operational efficiency.

As hybrid environments continue to evolve, the importance of effective identity management will only grow. Organizations that can successfully navigate the challenges of hybrid identity management will be better positioned to protect their assets, ensure compliance with regulatory requirements, and deliver a seamless and secure user experience. By embracing innovation and adopting best practices, organizations can build a resilient identity management framework that supports their digital transformation initiatives and drives success in an increasingly complex and interconnected world.

The Importance of Identity Auditing and Reporting

In the complex and ever-evolving landscape of cybersecurity, identity management has become a cornerstone of protecting organizational assets and data. While authentication, authorization, and access control mechanisms are critical to safeguarding sensitive information, these measures alone are not sufficient. To ensure that security policies are consistently enforced, regulatory requirements are met, and potential threats are promptly identified, organizations must implement robust identity auditing and reporting practices. These processes provide the visibility, accountability, and oversight necessary to manage digital identities effectively and maintain a strong security posture.

Identity auditing refers to the systematic process of reviewing and evaluating identity-related activities within an organization. This includes tracking user logins, access requests, permission changes, and other actions that involve identity and access management (IAM) systems. By maintaining detailed records of these activities, organizations can verify that access controls are functioning as intended, detect anomalies that may indicate security breaches, and demonstrate compliance with regulatory requirements. Identity auditing is not a one-time task but an ongoing process that requires continuous monitoring and analysis to ensure that identity-related risks are effectively managed.

One of the primary reasons identity auditing is essential is its role in ensuring compliance with regulatory and industry standards. Organizations across various sectors are subject to strict regulations that mandate the protection of sensitive data and the implementation of robust access controls. Regulations such as the General Data Protection Regulation (GDPR), the Health Insurance Portability and Accountability Act (HIPAA), the Sarbanes-Oxley Act (SOX), and the Payment Card Industry Data Security Standard (PCI DSS) require organizations to maintain detailed records of who accessed what data, when, and under what circumstances. Failure to comply with these regulations can result in severe legal and financial consequences, including fines, penalties, and reputational damage.

Identity auditing provides the evidence needed to demonstrate compliance during regulatory audits and assessments. By generating comprehensive audit logs and reports, organizations can show that they have implemented appropriate security measures, monitored access to sensitive data, and responded to potential security incidents in a timely manner. These records serve as proof that the organization has taken the necessary steps to protect its data and comply with legal requirements. Additionally, regular identity audits help identify gaps or weaknesses in access controls, allowing organizations to address these issues proactively before they result in compliance violations.

Beyond regulatory compliance, identity auditing plays a crucial role in enhancing overall security. By continuously monitoring identity-related activities, organizations can detect and respond to potential security threats more effectively. For example, if an employee who typically logs in from a specific geographic location suddenly accesses the system from an unfamiliar location or at an unusual time, the identity audit logs can flag this as suspicious behavior. Similarly, if a user attempts to access resources they do not typically use or makes multiple failed login attempts, these anomalies can indicate a potential security breach. By identifying such patterns early, organizations can take corrective actions, such as investigating the incident, revoking access, or implementing additional security measures.

Identity auditing also supports the principle of least privilege, which is a fundamental concept in cybersecurity. This principle dictates that users should have only the minimum level of access necessary to perform their job functions. Over time, however, users may accumulate additional permissions due to role changes, project assignments, or other factors. This phenomenon, known as privilege creep, increases the risk of unauthorized access and data breaches. Regular identity audits help organizations identify and rectify instances of privilege creep by reviewing user permissions and ensuring they align with current job responsibilities. By enforcing least privilege access, organizations can minimize the potential attack surface and reduce the likelihood of insider threats.

Another important aspect of identity auditing is its role in incident response and forensic investigations. When a security incident occurs, having access to detailed identity audit logs is invaluable for understanding the scope and impact of the breach. These logs provide a chronological record of user activities, allowing security teams to trace the actions of malicious actors, identify compromised accounts, and determine how the breach occurred. This information is critical for containing the incident, mitigating its effects, and preventing future occurrences. Additionally, audit logs can be used as evidence in legal proceedings, supporting efforts to hold perpetrators accountable and recover from the breach.

Identity reporting complements auditing by providing structured, actionable insights into identity-related activities and trends. While audit logs capture raw data, reports synthesize this information into meaningful summaries, visualizations, and metrics that can inform decision-making. Identity reports can highlight key performance indicators (KPIs), such as the number of access requests granted or denied, the frequency of failed login attempts, and the time taken to provision or de-provision user accounts. These metrics help organizations assess the effectiveness of their identity management practices, identify areas for improvement, and track progress over time.

Effective identity reporting also supports strategic planning and resource allocation. By analyzing identity-related data, organizations can identify patterns and trends that inform their cybersecurity strategies. For example, reports may reveal that certain departments or user groups are more prone to security incidents, prompting targeted training or additional security measures. Similarly, reports can highlight inefficiencies in access provisioning processes, leading to process improvements or investments in automation tools. By leveraging identity reporting, organizations can make data-driven decisions that enhance security, optimize operations, and support business goals.

Automation and advanced analytics play a significant role in modern identity auditing and reporting. As organizations generate vast amounts of identity-related data, manual review and analysis become impractical. Automated auditing tools can continuously monitor user activities, generate alerts for suspicious behavior, and produce regular reports without requiring constant human intervention. These tools often integrate with Security Information and Event Management

(SIEM) systems, providing a centralized platform for managing and analyzing security data. By leveraging automation, organizations can improve the efficiency and accuracy of their identity auditing and reporting processes, enabling faster detection and response to potential threats.

Artificial intelligence (AI) and machine learning (ML) further enhance identity auditing and reporting by enabling more sophisticated analysis of user behavior. AI-driven identity analytics can identify subtle anomalies and correlations that may be missed by traditional rule-based systems. For example, machine learning algorithms can analyze historical data to establish baseline behavior patterns for individual users and detect deviations that indicate potential security risks. By continuously learning from new data, these systems can adapt to evolving threats and improve their predictive capabilities over time. This proactive approach allows organizations to stay ahead of emerging risks and maintain a robust security posture.

Despite the many benefits of identity auditing and reporting, organizations must be mindful of potential challenges and limitations. One challenge is ensuring the integrity and security of audit logs and reports. Since these records contain sensitive information about user activities and access to critical systems, they are valuable targets for malicious actors seeking to cover their tracks or manipulate data. Organizations must implement strong security measures to protect audit logs, including encryption, access controls, and tamper-evident mechanisms. Additionally, maintaining the integrity of audit logs requires careful configuration and monitoring to prevent accidental deletion, corruption, or unauthorized modifications.

Another challenge is balancing the need for comprehensive auditing with privacy considerations. Identity audit logs often contain detailed information about user activities, raising concerns about employee privacy and data protection. Organizations must navigate these concerns by establishing clear policies and practices that balance security needs with respect for individual privacy. This includes defining the scope of auditing, ensuring transparency about data collection practices, and implementing measures to protect sensitive information. Compliance with data protection regulations, such as

GDPR, is essential to ensure that identity auditing practices align with legal and ethical standards.

The importance of identity auditing and reporting cannot be overstated in today's cybersecurity landscape. These practices provide the visibility, accountability, and oversight necessary to manage digital identities effectively, ensure compliance with regulatory requirements, and protect against security threats. By implementing robust auditing and reporting processes, organizations can detect and respond to potential risks, enforce access controls, and continuously improve their identity management practices. As technology continues to evolve and cyber threats become more sophisticated, identity auditing and reporting will remain essential tools for safeguarding organizational assets and maintaining trust in the digital world.

The Intersection of Identity and Privacy Laws (GDPR, CCPA)

In the digital age, where data drives decision-making and powers global economies, the intersection of identity management and privacy laws has become increasingly significant. Organizations today are entrusted with vast amounts of personal information, ranging from names and contact details to more sensitive data such as health records, financial transactions, and online behaviors. With the growing importance of protecting this data, governments worldwide have enacted robust privacy regulations to safeguard individual rights and ensure responsible data handling. Two of the most influential privacy laws—the General Data Protection Regulation (GDPR) in Europe and the California Consumer Privacy Act (CCPA) in the United States—have reshaped the landscape of identity management, compelling organizations to rethink how they collect, process, store, and protect personal information.

Identity management, at its core, is about ensuring that the right individuals have the right access to the right resources at the right time. It involves processes such as authentication, authorization, user provisioning, and access governance. However, identity management is not merely a technical concern; it is deeply intertwined with privacy principles. The way organizations manage digital identities directly impacts how personal data is protected, shared, and used. As privacy laws like GDPR and CCPA impose stringent requirements on data handling practices, identity management systems have become essential tools for achieving compliance and safeguarding individual privacy.

The General Data Protection Regulation (GDPR), which came into effect in May 2018, is one of the most comprehensive privacy laws globally, setting a high standard for data protection and privacy rights. It applies to any organization that processes the personal data of individuals within the European Union, regardless of where the organization is located. GDPR defines personal data broadly, encompassing any information that can identify an individual, either directly or indirectly. This includes obvious identifiers like names and email addresses, as well as IP addresses, location data, and even online behavioral information.

One of the core principles of GDPR is data minimization, which requires organizations to collect only the personal data that is necessary for a specific purpose. This principle has significant implications for identity management systems, which must be designed to limit data collection to what is strictly required for authentication and access control. For example, if a user needs to access a service, the organization should not collect additional data that is unrelated to that access. Identity management systems must also provide mechanisms for data anonymization and pseudonymization, ensuring that personal data is protected even if it is compromised.

GDPR also emphasizes the importance of transparency and user consent. Organizations are required to inform individuals about how their data will be used, who will have access to it, and how long it will be retained. Consent must be freely given, specific, informed, and unambiguous, and individuals have the right to withdraw their consent at any time. Identity management systems must be equipped to handle these requirements by providing clear communication about data usage and offering easy-to-use tools for managing consent. For example, user portals can allow individuals to view their data, adjust privacy settings, and revoke access permissions as needed.

Another critical aspect of GDPR is the principle of data subject rights, which grants individuals greater control over their personal data. These rights include the right to access, the right to rectification, the right to erasure (also known as the right to be forgotten), the right to data portability, and the right to object to data processing. Identity management systems play a crucial role in facilitating these rights by enabling organizations to quickly and accurately respond to data subject requests. For instance, when an individual requests to have their data deleted, the identity management system must ensure that all relevant data is securely erased from both active and backup systems.

Security is a central concern under GDPR, which mandates that organizations implement appropriate technical and organizational measures to protect personal data from unauthorized access, loss, or destruction. Identity and Access Management (IAM) solutions are critical to meeting these security requirements, as they control who can access personal data and under what conditions. Multi-Factor Authentication (MFA), role-based access control (RBAC), and continuous monitoring are just a few of the tools that organizations can use to enhance data security and demonstrate compliance with GDPR.

The California Consumer Privacy Act (CCPA), which took effect in January 2020, represents a landmark privacy law in the United States, granting California residents new rights over their personal data. While not as comprehensive as GDPR, CCPA shares many similarities, including a broad definition of personal information and a focus on transparency, user control, and data protection. CCPA applies to businesses that meet specific criteria, such as having annual gross revenues over $25 million, collecting personal data from 50,000 or more consumers, or deriving 50% or more of their revenue from selling personal information.

Under CCPA, consumers have the right to know what personal information is being collected, the purposes for which it is used, and with whom it is shared. They also have the right to request access to their data, request deletion of their data, and opt-out of the sale of their personal information. Identity management systems must support these rights by providing mechanisms for data access and deletion requests, as well as tools for managing data sharing preferences. For example, organizations can implement user dashboards that allow consumers to view their data, submit deletion requests, and opt-out of data sales with a simple click.

CCPA also introduces specific requirements for data security and breach notification. Businesses are required to implement reasonable security measures to protect personal information and must notify consumers in the event of a data breach. Identity management systems are essential for enforcing security policies and monitoring access to personal data. By implementing strong authentication methods, access controls, and audit logs, organizations can reduce the risk of data breaches and ensure that any incidents are quickly detected and addressed.

One of the unique aspects of CCPA is its focus on data monetization and the right to opt-out of data sales. Organizations that sell personal information must provide a clear and conspicuous "Do Not Sell My Personal Information" link on their websites, allowing consumers to opt-out easily. Identity management systems must integrate with these opt-out mechanisms to ensure that consumer preferences are respected across all data processing activities. This requires coordination between IAM systems, data management platforms, and third-party service providers to ensure that personal information is not sold or shared without proper consent.

The intersection of identity management and privacy laws like GDPR and CCPA highlights the growing importance of data governance in the digital age. Organizations must adopt a holistic approach to identity management that not only secures access to resources but also ensures compliance with privacy regulations and respects individual rights. This requires collaboration between IT, legal, compliance, and data governance teams to develop comprehensive policies and practices for managing personal data.

Technology alone is not sufficient to achieve compliance; organizations must also foster a culture of privacy and data protection. This involves educating employees about privacy principles, regularly reviewing and updating policies, and conducting audits to ensure that identity management practices align with legal requirements. By embedding privacy into the design of identity management systems and processes, organizations can build trust with consumers, mitigate risks, and demonstrate their commitment to responsible data handling.

As privacy laws continue to evolve and new regulations emerge, the intersection of identity management and privacy will become even more critical. Organizations must stay informed about legal developments, adapt their identity management strategies accordingly, and invest in technologies that support compliance and data protection. By doing so, they can navigate the complex landscape of digital identity and privacy, safeguard sensitive information, and uphold the rights of individuals in an increasingly connected world.

Mitigating Identity Theft and Fraud in the Digital Age

In today's interconnected world, the rise of digital platforms and services has revolutionized the way individuals and organizations interact, conduct business, and manage information. While these advancements have brought immense convenience and efficiency, they have also created fertile ground for identity theft and fraud. Cybercriminals are constantly developing new techniques to exploit vulnerabilities in digital systems, steal personal information, and commit fraud. As identity theft becomes more sophisticated and pervasive, mitigating its risks requires a comprehensive approach that combines technology, user education, and robust security practices.

Identity theft occurs when a malicious actor acquires and uses someone else's personal information, such as Social Security numbers, credit card details, or login credentials, to impersonate the victim for financial gain or other malicious purposes. The consequences of identity theft can be devastating, leading to financial loss, damaged reputations, and prolonged legal and administrative complications for victims. Fraud, closely related to identity theft, involves deceitful practices intended to secure unauthorized benefits or access. In the digital age, both identity theft and fraud can occur across a wide range of platforms, from e-commerce websites and social media accounts to banking systems and government databases.

One of the primary drivers of identity theft in the digital age is the sheer volume of personal information stored and shared online. Social media platforms, online shopping sites, financial institutions, and even healthcare providers collect vast amounts of sensitive data from users. This data, if not properly secured, becomes a prime target for cybercriminals. Data breaches, where large volumes of personal information are exposed due to vulnerabilities in security systems, have become alarmingly common. Once this data is stolen, it can be sold on the dark web or used directly to commit various forms of fraud, such as opening fraudulent accounts, making unauthorized purchases, or filing false tax returns.

Phishing is one of the most prevalent methods used by cybercriminals to steal personal information. In a phishing attack, the attacker sends fraudulent emails or messages that appear to come from legitimate sources, such as banks, government agencies, or well-known companies. These messages often contain links to fake websites designed to capture login credentials, credit card information, or other sensitive data. Spear-phishing, a more targeted form of phishing, focuses on specific individuals or organizations, using personalized information to increase the chances of success. Despite widespread awareness of phishing tactics, many people still fall victim due to the increasing sophistication of these schemes.

Another common vector for identity theft and fraud is malware—malicious software designed to infiltrate and compromise computer systems. Keyloggers, for instance, can record everything a user types, including passwords and personal information, while spyware secretly monitors and transmits data to cybercriminals. Ransomware, although primarily known for encrypting files and demanding payment, can also facilitate identity theft by stealing sensitive data before locking the system. With the proliferation of mobile devices, mobile malware has also become a significant threat, targeting smartphones and tablets to harvest personal information.

Mitigating identity theft and fraud in the digital age requires a multi-layered approach that addresses both technological and human factors. One of the most effective strategies is the implementation of strong authentication mechanisms. Multi-Factor Authentication (MFA) is a critical tool in this regard, requiring users to verify their identities using multiple factors, such as something they know (a password), something they have (a smartphone or security token), and something they are (biometric data like fingerprints or facial recognition). By adding these layers of security, MFA makes it significantly more difficult for cybercriminals to gain unauthorized access, even if they have obtained a user's password.

In addition to MFA, organizations and individuals should adopt robust password management practices. Passwords should be complex, unique, and changed regularly to minimize the risk of compromise. Password managers can help users generate and securely store strong passwords, reducing the likelihood of password reuse and simplifying the management of multiple credentials. Organizations should also enforce password policies that require complexity and regular updates, and they should monitor for signs of compromised credentials, such as those exposed in data breaches.

Encryption is another vital component of mitigating identity theft and fraud. Encrypting sensitive data ensures that even if it is intercepted or stolen, it cannot be easily read or used by unauthorized parties. Data should be encrypted both in transit and at rest, protecting information as it moves between systems and when it is stored on servers or devices. Secure communication protocols, such as HTTPS and Transport Layer Security (TLS), should be used to protect data transmitted over the internet, while strong encryption algorithms should safeguard stored data.

Monitoring and anomaly detection play a crucial role in identifying and responding to potential identity theft and fraud. Organizations should implement continuous monitoring systems that track user activities, detect unusual behavior, and generate alerts for suspicious actions. For example, if a user who typically logs in from a specific geographic location suddenly accesses the system from a foreign country or makes large transactions that deviate from their normal patterns, the system can flag these activities for further investigation. Behavioral analytics and machine learning can enhance these monitoring efforts by identifying subtle anomalies that may indicate fraudulent behavior.

User education and awareness are equally important in mitigating identity theft and fraud. Many cyberattacks rely on social engineering techniques that exploit human vulnerabilities rather than technical flaws. Educating users about common threats, such as phishing, malware, and social engineering tactics, can significantly reduce the likelihood of falling victim to these attacks. Organizations should conduct regular training sessions, simulated phishing exercises, and awareness campaigns to reinforce safe online practices and keep users informed about emerging threats.

Data minimization is another effective strategy for reducing the risk of identity theft. By collecting only the personal information necessary for specific purposes and retaining it for the shortest possible duration, organizations can limit the amount of data that could be exposed in the event of a breach. Implementing strict data access controls ensures that only authorized individuals have access to sensitive information, further reducing the risk of unauthorized exposure. Regular data audits can help identify and eliminate unnecessary or outdated information, minimizing the potential impact of a data breach.

Incident response planning is essential for mitigating the effects of identity theft and fraud when they do occur. Organizations should develop and maintain comprehensive incident response plans that outline the steps to be taken in the event of a security breach. This includes identifying and containing the breach, notifying affected individuals, cooperating with law enforcement, and implementing measures to prevent future incidents. Having a well-defined response plan ensures that organizations can react quickly and effectively to minimize the damage caused by identity theft and fraud.

Collaboration and information sharing are also critical in the fight against identity theft and fraud. Organizations, government agencies, and cybersecurity professionals must work together to share threat intelligence, identify emerging trends, and develop best practices for preventing and responding to attacks. Public-private partnerships, industry-specific information sharing organizations (ISACs), and cybersecurity alliances can facilitate this collaboration, enhancing the collective ability to combat identity-related threats.

As technology continues to evolve, so too will the tactics used by cybercriminals. The rise of artificial intelligence (AI) and machine learning presents both opportunities and challenges in this regard. While these technologies can be harnessed to improve security and detect fraudulent activities, they can also be used by attackers to develop more sophisticated and targeted attacks. Staying ahead of these evolving threats requires continuous innovation, investment in advanced security technologies, and a proactive approach to identity protection.

Ultimately, mitigating identity theft and fraud in the digital age is an ongoing effort that demands vigilance, adaptability, and a commitment to security at every level. By implementing strong authentication measures, adopting robust data protection practices, educating users, and fostering collaboration, organizations and individuals can significantly reduce their risk and build a more secure digital environment. As the digital landscape continues to expand, the importance of protecting identities and preventing fraud will remain a cornerstone of cybersecurity in the years to come.

The Future of Digital Identity: Trends and Predictions

As the digital world continues to expand, the concept of digital identity is undergoing rapid transformation. The traditional methods of managing identity, which often relied on static credentials like usernames and passwords, are increasingly inadequate in addressing the complexities of modern digital interactions. Emerging technologies, evolving cybersecurity threats, and shifting user expectations are all contributing to a new landscape for digital identity. The future of digital identity will be shaped by innovations that prioritize security, privacy, and user-centric control, while also accommodating the growing interconnectedness of our personal, professional, and civic lives.

One of the most prominent trends in the evolution of digital identity is the move toward passwordless authentication. Passwords have long been the weakest link in identity security, prone to being forgotten, reused, or stolen through phishing attacks and data breaches. As organizations seek to enhance security while improving user experience, passwordless solutions are gaining traction. These methods include biometric authentication, such as fingerprint scanning and facial recognition, as well as hardware tokens and mobile device-based authentication. By eliminating the need for passwords, these technologies reduce the risk of credential theft and simplify the login process for users.

Biometric authentication, in particular, is poised to play a significant role in the future of digital identity. The widespread adoption of smartphones and other personal devices equipped with biometric sensors has made it easier than ever to integrate biometric verification into everyday activities. Beyond fingerprints and facial recognition, emerging biometric technologies are exploring more advanced identifiers, such as voice recognition, retinal scans, and even behavioral biometrics, which analyze patterns like typing rhythm or gait. While biometrics offer enhanced security and convenience, they also raise concerns about privacy and data protection, particularly if biometric data is stored insecurely or used without proper consent.

Decentralized identity is another transformative trend that aims to give individuals greater control over their digital identities. Traditional identity systems are often centralized, with personal information stored and managed by a single entity, such as a government agency, financial institution, or technology company. This centralization creates vulnerabilities, as breaches can expose vast amounts of sensitive data. Decentralized identity frameworks, often built on blockchain technology, distribute control over identity data to the individuals themselves. Users can manage their credentials in secure digital wallets and share only the necessary information with service providers, reducing the risk of data breaches and enhancing privacy.

Self-sovereign identity (SSI) is a key concept within decentralized identity, emphasizing that individuals should own and control their personal data without relying on centralized authorities. SSI enables users to create and manage their digital identities independently, using cryptographic proofs to verify their credentials when needed. This approach not only enhances privacy and security but also simplifies identity verification processes across different contexts, from online banking and healthcare to voting and travel. As decentralized identity solutions mature, they have the potential to reshape how we think about identity in both the digital and physical worlds.

The integration of artificial intelligence (AI) and machine learning (ML) into digital identity systems is also shaping the future of identity management. AI-driven identity verification solutions can analyze large datasets to detect anomalies and identify fraudulent activities in real time. For example, AI can monitor login patterns, device usage, and user behavior to flag suspicious activities that may indicate identity theft or unauthorized access. Machine learning algorithms continuously adapt to new threats, improving the accuracy and effectiveness of identity verification processes. This proactive approach to identity security enables organizations to stay ahead of evolving cyber threats and reduce the risk of data breaches.

Another important development in the future of digital identity is the concept of identity federation and interoperability. As individuals and organizations interact with a growing number of digital platforms and services, the need for seamless and secure identity management across different systems becomes increasingly important. Federated identity systems allow users to authenticate once and access multiple services without needing to create separate credentials for each one. This approach not only simplifies the user experience but also enhances security by reducing the number of potential entry points for attackers. Interoperability between identity systems will be critical for enabling secure, frictionless interactions in an increasingly interconnected digital ecosystem.

The rise of the Internet of Things (IoT) is also influencing the future of digital identity. As more devices become connected to the internet—from smart home appliances and wearable technology to industrial sensors and autonomous vehicles—the need to manage and secure the identities of these devices becomes paramount. IoT identity management involves assigning unique digital identities to devices, ensuring they can authenticate and communicate securely within networks. This extends the principles of identity management beyond human users to include the vast array of connected devices that make up the modern digital landscape.

Privacy and data protection will remain central themes in the evolution of digital identity. With increasing awareness of data privacy issues and the growing regulatory landscape, such as the General Data Protection Regulation (GDPR) and the California Consumer Privacy Act (CCPA), organizations must prioritize the responsible handling of personal information. Privacy-by-design principles, which integrate privacy considerations into the development of identity management systems from the outset, will become standard practice. This includes minimizing data collection, implementing robust encryption, and providing users with greater transparency and control over their data.

Regulatory frameworks will continue to shape the future of digital identity, as governments and international bodies establish standards for identity verification, data protection, and cybersecurity. Digital identity initiatives, such as the European Union's eIDAS regulation and India's Aadhaar system, demonstrate the potential for government-led identity solutions to streamline services and improve access to resources. However, these initiatives also raise important questions about surveillance, data security, and the balance between convenience and individual rights. As digital identity systems become more widespread, policymakers will need to navigate these challenges to ensure that identity solutions are both secure and respectful of personal freedoms.

The convergence of digital identity with emerging technologies such as blockchain, AI, and IoT will create new opportunities and challenges in the years to come. Innovations like verifiable credentials, which allow individuals to prove specific attributes without revealing unnecessary personal information, will enhance privacy and reduce the risk of identity fraud. At the same time, the increasing sophistication of cyber threats will require continuous advancements in identity security, including the development of quantum-resistant cryptographic techniques to protect against future quantum computing threats.

The future of digital identity will also be shaped by shifting societal and cultural expectations. As digital interactions become more integral to our daily lives, individuals will demand greater control over their personal information and more transparent, user-friendly identity management solutions. Organizations that prioritize trust, security, and privacy in their identity practices will be better positioned to build lasting relationships with their customers and stakeholders. Moreover, the digital divide—differences in access to technology and digital literacy—will need to be addressed to ensure that digital identity solutions are inclusive and accessible to all individuals, regardless of their socioeconomic background.

In the years ahead, the evolution of digital identity will continue to be driven by the need for secure, efficient, and user-centric solutions that adapt to the changing digital landscape. The integration of advanced technologies, the emphasis on privacy and self-sovereign identity, and the growing importance of interoperability and regulatory compliance will all play key roles in shaping the future of identity management. By embracing these trends and staying ahead of emerging challenges, organizations and individuals can navigate the complexities of the digital age while ensuring that digital identities remain secure, private, and empowering.

Smart Devices and IoT: Expanding the Identity Landscape

The proliferation of smart devices and the Internet of Things (IoT) has revolutionized how individuals and organizations interact with technology. From smart homes and wearable devices to industrial sensors and connected vehicles, IoT has woven itself into nearly every aspect of modern life. While this rapid expansion has brought unprecedented convenience, efficiency, and innovation, it has also fundamentally transformed the landscape of identity management. The traditional concept of identity, once confined primarily to human users accessing digital systems, now encompasses a vast array of devices, each requiring secure authentication, authorization, and management. This shift has introduced new challenges and opportunities in the realm of identity security.

At its core, identity management is about ensuring that the right entities—whether human or machine—have access to the appropriate resources at the right time. In the context of IoT, this means that every connected device must have a unique digital identity to interact securely with other devices, networks, and systems. This is not a trivial task. The sheer number of devices, the diversity of manufacturers and platforms, and the varying levels of security capabilities make IoT identity management far more complex than traditional identity frameworks. Unlike human users, devices operate autonomously, often without direct human oversight, which necessitates automated, scalable, and robust identity solutions.

The expansion of the identity landscape to include smart devices begins with device authentication. Just as users authenticate themselves with passwords, biometrics, or tokens, devices must prove their identities to establish trust within a network. This is typically achieved through digital certificates, cryptographic keys, or hardware-based security modules. Public Key Infrastructure (PKI) plays a significant role in this process, providing a framework for issuing, managing, and validating digital certificates that authenticate devices. However, implementing PKI at scale for millions—or even billions—of devices presents logistical and technical challenges, including key management, certificate renewal, and revocation processes.

Once authenticated, devices must also be authorized to perform specific actions within a network. This involves defining what each device is allowed to do, which data it can access, and with which other devices it can communicate. Role-Based Access Control (RBAC) and Attribute-Based Access Control (ABAC) models, commonly used for human identity management, are being adapted for IoT environments. For instance, a smart thermostat may have the role of adjusting temperature settings within a home network, but it should not have access to sensitive data from a security camera. Ensuring that each device has the correct permissions requires meticulous planning and continuous monitoring to prevent unauthorized access or misuse.

The dynamic nature of IoT ecosystems adds another layer of complexity to identity management. Devices frequently join and leave networks, update their firmware, or change ownership. This constant flux necessitates robust identity lifecycle management processes that can handle device onboarding, configuration, updates, and decommissioning securely and efficiently. For example, when a smart device is sold or transferred to a new owner, its digital identity must be reset or reissued to prevent the previous owner from retaining access.

Similarly, when a device reaches the end of its lifecycle, its credentials must be securely revoked to prevent unauthorized use.

The security implications of poorly managed device identities are significant. IoT devices are often targeted by cybercriminals due to their vulnerabilities and the valuable data they collect. Insecure devices can be exploited to launch distributed denial-of-service (DDoS) attacks, infiltrate networks, or steal sensitive information. The infamous Mirai botnet attack in 2016, which hijacked thousands of IoT devices to disrupt major internet services, highlighted the potential scale and impact of such threats. Ensuring that each device has a secure, verifiable identity is crucial to mitigating these risks and protecting the integrity of IoT ecosystems.

In addition to security, privacy concerns are paramount in the expanding identity landscape. Many IoT devices collect and transmit personal data, from health metrics recorded by fitness trackers to location information gathered by smart vehicles. Managing the identities of these devices involves not only securing their communications but also ensuring compliance with data protection regulations such as the General Data Protection Regulation (GDPR) and the California Consumer Privacy Act (CCPA). This includes implementing measures for data minimization, user consent, and the right to access or delete personal information collected by IoT devices.

Interoperability is another critical consideration in IoT identity management. The IoT ecosystem comprises a wide variety of devices from different manufacturers, operating on diverse platforms and protocols. Ensuring that these devices can securely interact and exchange information requires standardized identity frameworks and protocols. Initiatives like the Open Connectivity Foundation (OCF) and the Industrial Internet Consortium (IIC) are working to establish common standards for IoT device identity and security. However, achieving widespread interoperability remains a challenge, particularly as new devices and technologies continue to emerge at a rapid pace.

Blockchain technology is increasingly being explored as a solution for managing IoT identities. By providing a decentralized and tamper-proof ledger, blockchain can facilitate secure and transparent identity verification and data sharing among devices. Each device can have a unique cryptographic identity recorded on the blockchain, ensuring that all interactions are traceable and verifiable. This approach reduces reliance on centralized authorities, enhancing security and resilience against attacks. However, the scalability and energy consumption of blockchain solutions remain concerns that must be addressed as these technologies mature.

Artificial intelligence (AI) and machine learning (ML) are also playing a growing role in IoT identity management. AI-driven analytics can monitor device behavior to detect anomalies and potential security threats in real time. For example, if a smart device suddenly begins communicating with unfamiliar endpoints or exhibits unusual data transmission patterns, AI algorithms can flag this behavior for further investigation or automatically initiate security protocols. Machine learning models can continuously adapt to new threats, improving the effectiveness of identity verification and access control mechanisms over time.

As the identity landscape expands to encompass smart devices and IoT, the role of identity governance becomes increasingly important. Organizations must implement comprehensive policies and procedures to manage device identities, enforce security standards, and ensure compliance with regulatory requirements. This includes regular audits of device access and activity, continuous monitoring for vulnerabilities, and prompt response to security incidents. Identity governance frameworks must also account for the unique challenges of IoT environments, such as the need for automated processes, scalable solutions, and real-time threat detection.

User education and awareness are essential components of effective IoT identity management. Many security vulnerabilities arise from user behaviors, such as failing to change default passwords, neglecting software updates, or misconfiguring device settings. Educating users about the importance of securing their smart devices, recognizing potential threats, and following best practices can significantly reduce the risk of identity-related incidents. This is particularly important in consumer IoT environments, where users may not have the same level of technical expertise as IT professionals in enterprise settings.

The future of identity management in the IoT era will be shaped by ongoing technological advancements, regulatory developments, and evolving user expectations. As the number and variety of connected devices continue to grow, so too will the complexity of managing their identities. Organizations and individuals alike must embrace innovative solutions, adopt best practices, and foster a culture of security and privacy to navigate this rapidly changing landscape. By doing so, they can harness the full potential of smart devices and IoT while safeguarding against the risks associated with an increasingly interconnected world.

The Role of Cryptography in Identity Protection

In the digital age, where data is exchanged at an unprecedented scale and pace, the protection of identities has become a cornerstone of cybersecurity. With the rise of online services, cloud computing, and interconnected devices, personal and organizational identities are constantly at risk of exposure, theft, and misuse. Cryptography, the science of securing information through mathematical techniques, plays a pivotal role in safeguarding these identities. It ensures that sensitive data remains confidential, authentic, and tamper-proof, providing the foundation for secure communication and trust in the digital world.

At its core, cryptography is about transforming information into a form that is unreadable to unauthorized parties while allowing intended recipients to access and interpret the data. This transformation is achieved through algorithms and keys that encrypt and decrypt information. In the context of identity protection, cryptography is used to secure personal data, authenticate users, and verify the integrity of communications and transactions. Without cryptographic techniques, the digital infrastructure that supports everything from online banking to secure email would be vulnerable to attacks, fraud, and breaches.

One of the primary applications of cryptography in identity protection is encryption. Encryption converts plaintext data into ciphertext, making it unintelligible to anyone who does not possess the correct decryption key. This ensures that personal information, such as social security numbers, credit card details, and login credentials, remains confidential even if intercepted by malicious actors. There are two main types of encryption used in identity protection: symmetric and asymmetric encryption.

Symmetric encryption uses a single key for both encryption and decryption. While this method is fast and efficient, it presents challenges in key distribution and management. If the key is compromised, so is the data it protects. Asymmetric encryption, on the other hand, uses a pair of keys: a public key for encryption and a private key for decryption. This method, also known as public-key cryptography, allows for secure communication without the need to share secret keys. Asymmetric encryption underpins many identity protection mechanisms, including digital certificates, secure email, and virtual private networks (VPNs).

Digital signatures are another critical cryptographic tool for identity protection. A digital signature is a mathematical scheme that verifies the authenticity and integrity of a message, document, or transaction. It uses asymmetric encryption to create a unique code that is linked to the sender's private key and the content being signed. The recipient can use the sender's public key to verify that the signature is valid and that the content has not been altered. Digital signatures are widely used in secure communications, software distribution, and legal documents, providing a high level of assurance that the information originates from a trusted source and has not been tampered with.

Public Key Infrastructure (PKI) is the framework that supports the use of public-key cryptography and digital signatures. PKI manages the issuance, distribution, and revocation of digital certificates, which bind public keys to the identities of individuals, organizations, or devices. Certificate Authorities (CAs) are trusted entities within the PKI that issue digital certificates after verifying the identity of the requester. When a user connects to a secure website, for example, the site's digital certificate is presented to the user's browser, which verifies its authenticity through the CA. This process, known as SSL/TLS, ensures that the website is legitimate and that any data exchanged is encrypted and secure.

Hash functions are another essential cryptographic technique used in identity protection. A hash function takes an input and produces a fixed-size string of characters, which appears random but is unique to the original input. Hash functions are designed to be one-way, meaning it is computationally infeasible to reverse the process and retrieve the original input from the hash value. In identity management, hash functions are commonly used to store passwords securely. Instead of storing plaintext passwords, systems store the hash values, and when a user attempts to log in, the system hashes the entered password and compares it to the stored hash. This approach ensures that even if the password database is compromised, the actual passwords remain protected.

Multi-Factor Authentication (MFA) relies heavily on cryptographic principles to enhance identity security. MFA requires users to provide multiple forms of verification before granting access to a system or service. These factors typically include something the user knows (a password), something the user has (a security token or smartphone), and something the user is (biometric data like fingerprints or facial recognition). Cryptographic techniques ensure that each factor is securely transmitted and verified, preventing unauthorized access even if one factor is compromised. For example, time-based one-time passwords (TOTPs), commonly used in MFA, are generated using cryptographic algorithms that synchronize with a server to produce temporary, unique codes.

In addition to securing individual identities, cryptography plays a crucial role in protecting the identities of devices and systems within networks. As the Internet of Things (IoT) continues to expand, each connected device requires a unique digital identity to authenticate and communicate securely with other devices and systems. Cryptographic techniques, such as digital certificates and secure key exchange protocols, ensure that these devices can be trusted and that their communications are protected from eavesdropping and tampering. This is particularly important in critical infrastructure sectors, such as healthcare, transportation, and energy, where the integrity and security of device identities are paramount.

Cryptographic techniques are also essential in protecting data privacy and ensuring compliance with data protection regulations, such as the

General Data Protection Regulation (GDPR) and the California Consumer Privacy Act (CCPA). These regulations mandate that organizations implement strong security measures to protect personal data from unauthorized access and breaches. Encryption, secure key management, and robust identity verification processes are critical components of meeting these regulatory requirements. By leveraging cryptography, organizations can demonstrate their commitment to data protection and reduce the risk of legal and financial penalties associated with data breaches.

Despite its critical role in identity protection, cryptography is not without its challenges. The strength of cryptographic systems depends on the robustness of the algorithms, the length of the keys, and the security of key management practices. As computational power increases, particularly with the advent of quantum computing, some current cryptographic algorithms may become vulnerable to attacks. Quantum computers have the potential to break widely used cryptographic methods, such as RSA and ECC (Elliptic Curve Cryptography), by solving complex mathematical problems much faster than classical computers. This has led to the development of post-quantum cryptography, which aims to create algorithms that are resistant to quantum attacks.

Another challenge is the proper implementation and management of cryptographic systems. Even the strongest algorithms can be rendered ineffective by poor key management, insecure storage, or flawed implementation. Organizations must ensure that cryptographic keys are generated, distributed, and stored securely, with strict access controls and regular audits. Additionally, staying up-to-date with the latest cryptographic standards and best practices is essential to maintaining robust identity protection.

As digital interactions become more complex and pervasive, the role of cryptography in identity protection will continue to grow. Emerging technologies, such as blockchain and decentralized identity systems, are leveraging cryptographic techniques to create more secure and user-centric models of identity management. Blockchain, for example, uses cryptographic hashing and digital signatures to create immutable records of transactions and identities, providing a high level of transparency and security. Decentralized identity frameworks give individuals greater control over their personal data, using cryptographic proofs to verify identities without relying on centralized authorities.

In the rapidly evolving digital landscape, cryptography remains the foundation of secure identity management. By ensuring the confidentiality, integrity, and authenticity of data and communications, cryptographic techniques protect individuals, organizations, and devices from identity theft, fraud, and unauthorized access. As new threats and technologies emerge, the continuous advancement and proper implementation of cryptographic methods will be essential to safeguarding digital identities and maintaining trust in the digital world.

Identity Management in Financial Services: A Case Study

The financial services sector stands at the forefront of digital transformation, balancing the need for seamless customer experiences with stringent security requirements. With the growing adoption of online banking, mobile payments, and digital financial products, effective identity management has become a cornerstone of trust and operational efficiency in this industry. Financial institutions are responsible for protecting sensitive customer data, ensuring compliance with regulatory mandates, and preventing fraud—all while maintaining user-friendly access to services. This case study explores how a mid-sized bank successfully implemented a robust identity management system, highlighting the challenges faced, solutions adopted, and outcomes achieved.

The bank in question, referred to here as "FinSecure Bank," operates in multiple regions, offering a range of financial products including personal banking, loans, and investment services. As the bank expanded its digital offerings, it encountered significant challenges related to identity management. Customers expected secure, convenient access to their accounts across various platforms, while regulatory bodies imposed strict compliance requirements such as the General Data Protection Regulation (GDPR), the Payment Card Industry Data Security Standard (PCI DSS), and Know Your Customer

(KYC) regulations. Additionally, the bank faced rising threats from cybercriminals attempting to exploit identity-related vulnerabilities.

Before implementing a new identity management system, FinSecure Bank relied on a patchwork of legacy systems that lacked integration and scalability. Different departments managed identities separately, leading to inconsistent access controls and redundant user data. Customers often had to create multiple login credentials for different services, resulting in poor user experiences and increased support requests due to forgotten passwords or locked accounts. Internally, the bank struggled with managing employee access to sensitive data, increasing the risk of insider threats and unauthorized access.

Recognizing the need for a comprehensive solution, FinSecure Bank embarked on a project to overhaul its identity management framework. The bank's primary objectives were to unify customer and employee identities under a centralized system, enhance security through multi-factor authentication (MFA), streamline compliance with regulatory requirements, and improve the overall user experience. To achieve these goals, the bank partnered with a leading identity and access management (IAM) solutions provider, selecting a cloud-based platform capable of integrating with existing systems and scaling with future growth.

The first phase of the implementation focused on consolidating customer identities into a single, unified profile. This involved migrating data from disparate systems, standardizing identity attributes, and establishing a master identity repository. By creating a single source of truth for customer identities, the bank could offer a seamless, consistent experience across all digital channels. Customers were provided with a unified login that granted access to online banking, mobile apps, and investment platforms, eliminating the need for multiple credentials. This not only improved user convenience but also reduced the administrative burden on support teams.

To enhance security, FinSecure Bank integrated multi-factor authentication into its identity management system. Customers were required to verify their identities using two or more authentication factors, such as a password combined with a one-time passcode sent to their mobile device or biometric verification through fingerprint or facial recognition. MFA significantly reduced the risk of unauthorized access, even if a user's credentials were compromised. The bank also implemented risk-based authentication, which adjusted security measures based on the context of the login attempt. For example, if a customer attempted to access their account from an unfamiliar location or device, additional verification steps were triggered to ensure the legitimacy of the request.

Internally, the bank adopted role-based access control (RBAC) to manage employee access to sensitive data and systems. By assigning roles based on job functions, the bank ensured that employees had access only to the information necessary for their responsibilities, minimizing the risk of data breaches and insider threats. The IAM system also automated the provisioning and de-provisioning of employee accounts, streamlining the onboarding and offboarding processes. When an employee joined the bank, their access rights were automatically assigned based on their role, and when they left, their access was promptly revoked, reducing the risk of orphaned accounts.

Compliance with regulatory requirements was a critical consideration throughout the implementation process. The IAM platform provided built-in tools for managing and documenting access controls, supporting the bank's efforts to meet GDPR, PCI DSS, and KYC mandates. For instance, the system maintained detailed audit logs of all identity-related activities, enabling the bank to track who accessed what data, when, and under what circumstances. These logs were essential for demonstrating compliance during regulatory audits and for investigating potential security incidents.

To further support compliance, the bank implemented identity governance features that facilitated regular access reviews and certification processes. Managers were required to periodically review and certify employee access to sensitive data, ensuring that permissions remained appropriate and aligned with current job responsibilities. This process helped identify and address privilege creep, where users accumulate excessive access rights over time, posing a security risk.

The integration of customer and employee identities under a unified system also enabled the bank to leverage advanced analytics for fraud detection and prevention. By analyzing patterns of user behavior, the IAM platform could identify anomalies that might indicate fraudulent activities. For example, if a customer who typically accessed their account from a specific geographic region suddenly initiated transactions from a foreign country, the system could flag this behavior for further investigation. Similarly, unusual patterns of employee access to sensitive data could trigger alerts, enabling the bank to respond proactively to potential threats.

The implementation of the new identity management system delivered significant benefits for FinSecure Bank. Customers enjoyed a seamless, secure experience across all digital channels, leading to increased satisfaction and loyalty. The adoption of multi-factor authentication and risk-based access controls significantly reduced the incidence of unauthorized access and fraud. Internally, the bank achieved greater efficiency in managing employee identities, reducing administrative overhead and improving security through automated provisioning and role-based access control.

From a compliance perspective, the bank was better positioned to meet regulatory requirements and respond to audits with confidence. The detailed audit logs, automated access reviews, and robust identity governance processes provided clear evidence of the bank's commitment to data protection and regulatory compliance. This not only mitigated the risk of legal and financial penalties but also enhanced the bank's reputation as a trustworthy and secure financial institution.

The success of the identity management implementation at FinSecure Bank highlights several key lessons for other organizations in the financial services sector. First, the importance of a centralized, unified identity management system cannot be overstated. By consolidating identities and standardizing access controls, organizations can improve security, streamline operations, and enhance user experiences. Second, the integration of multi-factor authentication and risk-based access controls is essential for protecting against the growing threat of cyberattacks and fraud. These measures provide an additional layer of security that is critical in today's digital landscape.

Third, regulatory compliance should be a central consideration in any identity management initiative. Financial institutions operate in a highly regulated environment, and failure to meet compliance requirements can have severe consequences. Implementing tools and processes that support compliance, such as audit logs, access reviews, and identity governance, is essential for mitigating risk and demonstrating accountability.

Finally, the case study underscores the value of leveraging advanced analytics and automation in identity management. By continuously monitoring user behavior and automating routine processes, organizations can detect and respond to potential threats more effectively, while also improving operational efficiency.

As the financial services industry continues to evolve, identity management will remain a critical component of cybersecurity and operational strategy. The successful implementation at FinSecure Bank serves as a model for how financial institutions can navigate the complexities of digital identity, protect sensitive data, and build trust with customers in an increasingly interconnected world.

Healthcare and Identity Security: Protecting Sensitive Data

In the healthcare industry, the protection of sensitive data is not just a matter of privacy—it's a critical component of patient safety and trust. With the digitization of medical records, telemedicine, and interconnected healthcare systems, safeguarding patient identities has become a complex challenge. Healthcare organizations are prime targets for cybercriminals due to the vast amount of personal and medical data they store, from Social Security numbers and insurance details to medical histories and prescription records. This data, if compromised, can lead to identity theft, financial fraud, and even life-threatening consequences if medical records are altered. Ensuring robust identity security in healthcare is essential for protecting patient information, complying with regulations, and maintaining the integrity of healthcare services.

Healthcare data breaches are increasingly common, and their impacts are far-reaching. Unlike financial information, which can often be changed or canceled, medical information is permanent. Once exposed, sensitive health data can be used to commit medical identity theft, where fraudsters use stolen information to obtain medical services, prescriptions, or insurance benefits. This not only leads to financial losses for victims and healthcare providers but can also result in incorrect medical records, posing serious risks to patient health. For example, if a fraudulent medical procedure is added to a patient's record, it could lead to incorrect treatments or prescriptions in the future.

The shift to electronic health records (EHRs) and the growing adoption of telehealth services have significantly expanded the digital footprint of healthcare organizations. While these advancements improve efficiency, accessibility, and patient care, they also create new vulnerabilities. Healthcare providers must manage and secure a vast array of digital identities, including patients, healthcare professionals, administrative staff, and third-party vendors. Each of these identities requires controlled access to different systems and data, making identity management a critical aspect of healthcare cybersecurity.

One of the fundamental principles of identity security in healthcare is ensuring that the right individuals have access to the right information at the right time. This is achieved through robust identity and access management (IAM) systems that authenticate users and authorize their access based on predefined roles and responsibilities. Role-based access control (RBAC) is widely used in healthcare to ensure that employees can only access the information necessary for their job functions. For instance, a nurse might have access to patient care records but not to billing information, while an administrative staff member might access scheduling systems but not medical histories.

Multi-factor authentication (MFA) is another critical tool in healthcare identity security. By requiring users to verify their identities using multiple methods—such as a password combined with a fingerprint scan or a one-time code sent to a mobile device—MFA adds an extra layer of protection against unauthorized access. This is particularly important in healthcare, where stolen credentials can provide access to highly sensitive information. Implementing MFA across all systems, including EHR platforms and remote access tools, helps mitigate the risk of data breaches and unauthorized access.

Healthcare organizations must also navigate a complex regulatory landscape that mandates strict data protection measures. In the United States, the Health Insurance Portability and Accountability Act (HIPAA) sets the standard for protecting sensitive patient information. HIPAA requires healthcare providers to implement administrative, physical, and technical safeguards to ensure the confidentiality, integrity, and availability of protected health information (PHI). This includes measures for secure authentication, access controls, audit logging, and data encryption. Non-compliance with HIPAA can result in severe financial penalties and legal consequences, as well as damage to an organization's reputation.

Beyond HIPAA, healthcare organizations must also comply with other regulations and standards, such as the General Data Protection Regulation (GDPR) in the European Union, which governs the handling of personal data, including health information. GDPR emphasizes the importance of data minimization, requiring organizations to collect only the data necessary for specific purposes, and mandates that individuals have control over their personal information. This includes the right to access, correct, and delete their data, as well as the right to be informed about how their data is used. Compliance with GDPR and similar regulations requires healthcare organizations to implement comprehensive data governance and identity management practices.

The complexity of healthcare environments presents unique challenges for identity security. Hospitals, clinics, and other healthcare facilities often rely on a mix of legacy systems and modern technologies, making it difficult to implement consistent security measures across all platforms. Additionally, healthcare professionals frequently move between departments, facilities, and even organizations, requiring flexible and dynamic identity management solutions. The need for quick and seamless access to patient information in emergency situations further complicates the balance between security and usability.

To address these challenges, many healthcare organizations are adopting federated identity management systems. Federated identity allows users to access multiple systems and applications with a single set of credentials, streamlining the authentication process and reducing the risk of password-related security issues. This is particularly valuable in healthcare, where professionals may need to access systems across different hospitals, clinics, and partner organizations. Federated identity management improves both security and efficiency by centralizing identity verification and reducing the need for multiple logins.

Another emerging trend in healthcare identity security is the use of biometric authentication. Biometric technologies, such as fingerprint scanning, facial recognition, and iris scanning, provide a secure and convenient method for verifying identities. In healthcare settings, biometrics can be used to authenticate both patients and healthcare providers, ensuring that only authorized individuals have access to sensitive information and medical equipment. For example, biometric authentication can be used to secure access to medication dispensing systems, reducing the risk of medication errors and unauthorized use.

The integration of artificial intelligence (AI) and machine learning (ML) into healthcare identity security is also gaining traction. AI-driven systems can analyze patterns of user behavior to detect anomalies that may indicate security threats. For example, if a healthcare professional accesses patient records outside of normal working hours or from an unusual location, the system can flag this activity for further investigation. Machine learning algorithms can continuously adapt to new threats, improving the accuracy and effectiveness of identity verification processes over time. This proactive approach to identity security helps healthcare organizations stay ahead of evolving cyber threats.

In addition to securing digital identities, healthcare organizations must also protect the physical security of sensitive information. This includes implementing measures to prevent unauthorized access to physical records, devices, and facilities. For example, access to secure areas, such as data centers and record storage rooms, should be restricted to authorized personnel through the use of key cards, biometric scanners, or other access control systems. Physical security measures must be integrated with digital identity management systems to provide a comprehensive approach to protecting sensitive data.

Patient education and engagement are also critical components of healthcare identity security. Patients play an active role in protecting their own health information, and healthcare providers must ensure that they are informed about best practices for safeguarding their data. This includes educating patients on the importance of strong, unique passwords for accessing patient portals, recognizing phishing attempts, and understanding their rights under data protection regulations. By fostering a culture of security awareness among both patients and staff, healthcare organizations can create a more resilient defense against identity-related threats.

The COVID-19 pandemic has further underscored the importance of robust identity security in healthcare. The rapid shift to telehealth services and remote work for healthcare professionals has expanded the attack surface for cybercriminals. Ensuring secure access to telehealth platforms, protecting patient data during virtual consultations, and safeguarding remote access to healthcare systems have become top priorities. The pandemic has accelerated the adoption of digital health technologies, highlighting the need for scalable and adaptable identity management solutions that can keep pace with changing healthcare delivery models.

As healthcare continues to evolve in the digital age, the importance of identity security will only grow. Protecting sensitive patient data is essential not only for compliance and operational efficiency but also for maintaining the trust and confidence of patients. By implementing comprehensive identity and access management strategies, leveraging advanced technologies, and fostering a culture of security awareness, healthcare organizations can safeguard their data, protect their patients, and ensure the integrity of their services in an increasingly connected world.

Government and Citizen Identity: National ID Programs

In the modern world, the relationship between governments and citizens is increasingly mediated through digital systems. National ID programs play a pivotal role in this dynamic, serving as the foundation for a wide range of public and private services, from voting and healthcare to banking and social welfare. These programs aim to provide secure, reliable, and universally recognized forms of identification that streamline interactions between individuals and state institutions. While national ID systems offer numerous benefits in terms of efficiency, security, and inclusivity, they also raise critical questions about privacy, data protection, and the potential for government overreach.

National ID programs are designed to establish a unique and verifiable identity for every citizen and, in some cases, residents and visitors. This identity is typically tied to a physical document, such as a card or passport, that contains personal information and, increasingly, biometric data. In many countries, these IDs are integrated into broader digital identity frameworks that allow for online authentication and access to electronic government (e-government) services. The objective is to create a seamless identity management system that simplifies administrative processes, reduces fraud, and enhances the delivery of public services.

One of the most prominent examples of a national ID program is India's Aadhaar system, which has enrolled over a billion people since its inception. Aadhaar assigns a unique 12-digit identification number to each individual, linked to their biometric data, including fingerprints and iris scans. This system has been instrumental in streamlining the distribution of social welfare benefits, reducing corruption, and enabling financial inclusion for previously unbanked populations. Aadhaar's digital identity infrastructure allows individuals to verify their identities online, facilitating access to a wide range of services, from opening bank accounts to receiving government subsidies.

Similarly, Estonia has garnered international attention for its advanced e-Residency and national ID card programs. Every Estonian citizen is issued a digital ID card that provides secure access to over 600 e-services, including voting, tax filing, and medical records. Estonia's digital identity system is built on a robust public key infrastructure (PKI) that ensures the security and integrity of online transactions. The country's e-Residency program extends these benefits to non-citizens, allowing entrepreneurs worldwide to establish and manage businesses within the European Union without being physically present in Estonia.

While national ID programs offer significant advantages in terms of efficiency and accessibility, they also present substantial challenges related to privacy and data security. Centralizing vast amounts of personal information in government databases creates attractive targets for cybercriminals and increases the risk of data breaches. The inclusion of biometric data, which is immutable and uniquely tied to an individual, adds an additional layer of complexity. Unlike passwords or other credentials, biometric data cannot be changed if compromised, making its protection paramount.

Privacy advocates have raised concerns about the potential for national ID programs to enable mass surveillance and infringe on individual freedoms. The centralization of identity data can give governments unprecedented access to personal information, raising fears about misuse or abuse of power. In countries with weak data protection laws or authoritarian regimes, national ID systems can be used to monitor political dissent, restrict access to services based on discriminatory practices, or even facilitate human rights abuses. Balancing the benefits of national ID programs with the need to protect civil liberties is a critical challenge for policymakers and technologists alike.

To address these concerns, many countries have implemented strict legal and technical safeguards to protect the integrity and privacy of national ID systems. The European Union's General Data Protection Regulation (GDPR) sets a high standard for data protection, requiring transparency, accountability, and user consent in the handling of personal information. National ID programs within the EU must comply with these regulations, ensuring that citizens have control over their data and that appropriate measures are in place to prevent unauthorized access or misuse.

Technological innovations are also playing a role in enhancing the security and privacy of national ID systems. Decentralized identity frameworks, which leverage blockchain and other distributed ledger technologies, offer an alternative to traditional centralized databases. In decentralized systems, individuals retain control over their identity data, sharing only the information necessary for specific transactions. This approach reduces the risk of large-scale data breaches and enhances privacy by minimizing the amount of personal information stored in central repositories.

For example, the concept of self-sovereign identity (SSI) empowers individuals to manage their digital identities independently of government or corporate entities. SSI systems use cryptographic proofs to verify identity attributes without revealing unnecessary personal information. A citizen could prove they are of legal voting age without disclosing their exact birthdate, or verify their residency status without sharing their full address. By putting individuals in control of their own data, SSI frameworks aim to enhance trust and privacy in digital identity systems.

The implementation of national ID programs also raises important questions about inclusivity and accessibility. While these systems are often designed to streamline access to public services, they can inadvertently exclude marginalized populations who lack the necessary documentation or technological resources. For example, undocumented immigrants, homeless individuals, and people living in remote areas may face significant barriers in enrolling in national ID programs. Ensuring that these systems are inclusive and equitable requires thoughtful design and outreach efforts, as well as alternative mechanisms for identity verification that accommodate diverse populations.

In some cases, national ID programs have been criticized for exacerbating existing inequalities. For instance, while India's Aadhaar system has successfully enrolled a large portion of the population, there have been reports of individuals being denied access to essential services due to authentication failures or discrepancies in their identity records. Biometric systems can sometimes struggle with accuracy, particularly for individuals with worn fingerprints, disabilities, or other characteristics that affect the reliability of biometric scans. Addressing these challenges requires continuous refinement of the technology and robust mechanisms for individuals to challenge and correct errors in their records.

The global proliferation of national ID programs highlights the need for international standards and cooperation in the realm of digital identity. As people increasingly cross borders for work, study, and travel, the ability to verify identities across different national systems becomes critical. Efforts such as the United Nations' Sustainable Development Goal 16.9, which aims to provide legal identity for all by 2030, underscore the importance of inclusive and secure identity systems on a global scale. International organizations, governments, and technology providers must collaborate to establish interoperable standards that protect individual rights while facilitating cross-border interactions.

In the future, national ID programs are likely to become even more integrated with emerging technologies and digital ecosystems. The rise of smart cities, connected healthcare, and digital finance will create new opportunities and challenges for identity management. Ensuring that national ID systems can adapt to these evolving contexts while maintaining security, privacy, and inclusivity will be essential. Moreover, as artificial intelligence and big data analytics become more prevalent, governments must be vigilant in safeguarding against the misuse of identity data and ensuring that these technologies are deployed ethically and responsibly.

Ultimately, the success of national ID programs hinges on building and maintaining public trust. Transparent governance, strong legal protections, and robust technological safeguards are essential for ensuring that these systems serve the public good without compromising individual freedoms. By prioritizing privacy, security, and inclusivity, governments can create identity systems that not only enhance administrative efficiency but also empower citizens and strengthen democratic institutions in an increasingly digital world.

Educational Institutions and Student Identity Management

In the evolving landscape of education, managing student identities has become a complex yet crucial task. As educational institutions increasingly adopt digital platforms for learning, administration, and communication, the need for secure, efficient, and flexible identity management systems has never been more critical. Student identity management encompasses a range of processes, from enrollment and authentication to access control and data protection. It ensures that the right individuals have access to the appropriate resources while safeguarding sensitive information and complying with regulatory requirements. The challenges and opportunities in this area highlight the importance of robust identity management frameworks in fostering a secure and effective educational environment.

Student identity management begins at the point of admission, where institutions collect and verify personal information to create unique digital identities for each student. This identity typically includes basic demographic data, academic records, and credentials for accessing online platforms. As students progress through their educational journey, their digital identities evolve to reflect changes in enrollment status, course registrations, and extracurricular activities. Managing this lifecycle requires a comprehensive approach that integrates various systems and ensures consistent, accurate, and secure handling of student data.

One of the primary challenges in student identity management is balancing security with accessibility. Educational institutions must protect sensitive information, such as Social Security numbers, financial aid records, and health data, while providing seamless access to academic resources. Students need to log into learning management systems (LMS), library databases, and campus portals without unnecessary friction, especially as remote and hybrid learning models become more prevalent. Achieving this balance requires implementing robust authentication mechanisms that verify student identities without compromising user experience.

Multi-factor authentication (MFA) is a key tool in enhancing the security of student identity management systems. By requiring students to provide multiple forms of verification—such as a password combined with a one-time code sent to their mobile device or biometric authentication like fingerprint or facial recognition—MFA significantly reduces the risk of unauthorized access. This is particularly important in preventing account breaches that could expose personal information or disrupt academic activities. While MFA adds an extra layer of security, it must be designed to minimize inconvenience, ensuring that students can easily and reliably access the resources they need.

Single sign-on (SSO) solutions further streamline student access to educational platforms. With SSO, students can log in once to access multiple applications and services, eliminating the need to remember multiple usernames and passwords. This not only improves the user experience but also reduces the likelihood of password-related security issues, such as weak passwords or credential reuse. Implementing SSO requires integrating diverse systems, from LMS platforms and email services to third-party educational tools, under a unified identity management framework.

Educational institutions also face the challenge of managing diverse user groups with varying access needs. In addition to students, these institutions must manage identities for faculty, staff, alumni, and external partners. Each group requires different levels of access to resources, and these permissions may change over time. Role-based access control (RBAC) is commonly used to address this complexity, assigning access rights based on predefined roles within the institution. For example, a student may have access to course materials and academic records, while a faculty member can access grading systems and research databases. RBAC simplifies the management of permissions and ensures that users can only access information relevant to their roles.

The lifecycle management of student identities extends beyond the classroom. Alumni often retain access to certain institutional resources, such as library databases or career services, long after graduation. Managing these ongoing relationships requires systems that can adjust access rights based on changes in status while maintaining the integrity of historical academic records. This includes deactivating accounts when necessary to prevent unauthorized access and ensuring that alumni data is securely stored and protected.

Data privacy is a critical concern in student identity management. Educational institutions are custodians of vast amounts of personal information, and they must comply with legal frameworks that govern data protection. In the United States, the Family Educational Rights and Privacy Act (FERPA) establishes guidelines for the access and disclosure of student educational records. FERPA grants students the right to access their records, request corrections, and control the disclosure of their information to third parties. Compliance with FERPA requires institutions to implement stringent data security measures and to educate staff and faculty about privacy policies and procedures.

Globally, other regulations, such as the General Data Protection Regulation (GDPR) in the European Union, impose additional requirements on institutions that handle the personal data of students from affected regions. GDPR emphasizes transparency, data minimization, and the right to be forgotten, requiring institutions to provide clear information about data usage and to delete personal data upon request when it is no longer necessary. Navigating these regulatory landscapes requires a proactive approach to data governance, ensuring that student identity management systems align with legal and ethical standards.

The increasing use of cloud-based services and third-party applications in education introduces additional complexities in student identity management. Institutions must ensure that these external platforms comply with data protection standards and that student data is securely transmitted and stored. Vendor management and due diligence are critical in this context, as institutions must evaluate the security practices of third-party providers and establish clear agreements regarding data handling and privacy. Integrating these services with institutional identity management systems requires careful planning to maintain consistent access controls and data integrity.

Artificial intelligence (AI) and machine learning (ML) are emerging as powerful tools in student identity management. AI-driven analytics can monitor user behavior to detect anomalies that may indicate security threats, such as unusual login patterns or unauthorized access attempts. Machine learning algorithms can adapt to evolving threats, improving the accuracy of identity verification processes over time. Additionally, AI can enhance the personalization of educational experiences by leveraging identity data to tailor learning resources, track academic progress, and provide targeted support to students.

The role of biometric authentication in student identity management is also expanding. Biometric technologies, such as fingerprint scanning, facial recognition, and voice authentication, offer a secure and convenient method for verifying identities. These technologies can be used for various purposes, from accessing campus facilities and electronic devices to taking online exams and submitting assignments. While biometrics enhance security, they also raise concerns about privacy and data protection, particularly regarding the storage and handling of sensitive biometric data. Institutions must implement robust safeguards to protect biometric information and ensure compliance with relevant privacy regulations.

The COVID-19 pandemic has accelerated the adoption of digital identity management solutions in education. With the shift to remote learning, institutions have faced increased pressure to secure online platforms and protect student data in virtual environments. The need for reliable identity verification in online exams and assessments has driven the development of advanced proctoring solutions that combine biometric authentication, AI monitoring, and secure browser technologies. While these tools help maintain academic integrity, they also raise questions about student privacy and the ethical implications of surveillance in educational settings.

Collaboration and interoperability are essential for effective student identity management, particularly in institutions with complex organizational structures or partnerships with other educational entities. Federated identity management systems allow institutions to establish trust relationships with external partners, enabling students to access resources across different campuses, consortia, or international programs with a single set of credentials. This approach facilitates academic collaboration and mobility while maintaining consistent security and access controls.

As technology continues to evolve, educational institutions must remain agile in their approach to student identity management. Continuous investment in security infrastructure, staff training, and policy development is essential to address emerging threats and challenges. Institutions must also engage with students as active participants in identity management, educating them about best practices for protecting their personal information and navigating digital platforms securely.

In the future, the convergence of technologies such as blockchain, decentralized identity frameworks, and advanced biometrics may redefine how educational institutions manage student identities. These innovations have the potential to enhance security, streamline administrative processes, and empower students with greater control over their personal data. By embracing these advancements and prioritizing privacy, security, and inclusivity, educational institutions can create a resilient identity management framework that supports academic success and fosters trust in the digital age.

Balancing User Experience and Security in Identity Systems

In today's digital landscape, identity systems are fundamental to how users access and interact with online platforms and services. From social media and e-commerce to banking and enterprise applications, identity management plays a critical role in securing data and ensuring that only authorized individuals can access sensitive information. However, as the need for robust security measures grows in response to rising cyber threats, organizations face the challenge of balancing security with user experience. While strong security protocols are essential, overly complex systems can frustrate users, leading to reduced engagement, poor satisfaction, and even insecure workarounds. Finding the right equilibrium between user convenience and stringent security is essential for building effective, trustworthy identity systems.

The tension between user experience (UX) and security arises because the goals of each can often seem at odds. Security measures are designed to protect data, authenticate users, and prevent unauthorized access, often requiring multiple verification steps, complex passwords, and strict access controls. Conversely, users expect quick, seamless, and intuitive access to services, without unnecessary hurdles or delays. If security protocols are too cumbersome, users may feel hindered, potentially abandoning the service or finding ways to bypass security measures altogether. On the other hand, prioritizing convenience at the expense of security can leave systems vulnerable to attacks, data breaches, and identity theft.

One of the most common areas where this balance is tested is in password management. Traditional identity systems rely heavily on passwords as the primary method of authentication. However, passwords are often a weak link in security, as users tend to choose simple, easily guessable passwords or reuse the same credentials across multiple platforms. To mitigate these risks, organizations may enforce complex password requirements, such as a mix of uppercase and lowercase letters, numbers, and special characters, along with frequent password changes. While these measures enhance security, they also increase cognitive load on users, making it harder for them to remember their credentials. This can lead to poor practices like writing down passwords, using predictable patterns, or relying on password reset features, all of which undermine security.

To address these challenges, many organizations are adopting passwordless authentication methods, which both enhance security and improve user experience. Technologies such as biometrics (fingerprint scanning, facial recognition, voice recognition), hardware security keys, and one-time passcodes (OTPs) sent to mobile devices offer secure alternatives to traditional passwords. These methods reduce the reliance on user-generated credentials while providing a more streamlined and intuitive login process. For instance, using a fingerprint to unlock an account is faster and easier for users while offering a higher level of security than a traditional password. Passwordless authentication thus represents a significant step toward harmonizing security and usability.

Multi-factor authentication (MFA) is another crucial security measure that, when implemented thoughtfully, can balance protection with user convenience. MFA requires users to verify their identity through multiple factors, typically combining something they know (a password), something they have (a mobile device or security token), and something they are (biometric data). While MFA significantly strengthens security by adding layers of verification, poorly designed MFA systems can frustrate users, particularly if they involve cumbersome steps or frequent prompts. To enhance user experience, organizations can adopt adaptive or risk-based MFA, which adjusts the level of authentication required based on the context of the login attempt. For example, if a user logs in from a recognized device and location, the system might require only a single factor, while an unfamiliar login from a new location might trigger full MFA. This dynamic approach maintains strong security without imposing unnecessary friction on users.

Single sign-on (SSO) solutions also play a pivotal role in balancing security and user experience. SSO allows users to authenticate once and gain access to multiple applications and services without needing to log in separately to each one. This not only simplifies the login process for users but also reduces the number of credentials they need to manage, decreasing the risk of password fatigue and insecure practices. From a security perspective, SSO centralizes authentication, enabling more consistent enforcement of security policies and easier monitoring of access activities. However, because SSO systems create a single point of entry, it is crucial to implement strong security measures, such as robust MFA, to protect the initial authentication process.

User interface (UI) and user experience (UX) design also play significant roles in how identity systems are perceived and used. Clear, intuitive interfaces can guide users through secure authentication processes without confusion or frustration. For example, providing clear instructions for creating strong passwords, offering visual feedback on password strength, and simplifying the steps for setting up MFA can enhance both security and usability. Error messages and prompts should be designed to help users recover from mistakes without compromising security, such as offering secure options for account recovery without revealing sensitive information. Thoughtful design can reduce user errors, increase engagement, and foster trust in the identity system.

Transparency and user control are critical components of building trust and balancing security with user experience. Users should be informed about how their data is collected, stored, and used, and they should have control over their personal information. Providing clear privacy policies, offering easy-to-use settings for managing data permissions, and enabling users to view and revoke access to connected applications are ways to enhance transparency and empower users. When users feel that they have control over their data and understand the security measures in place, they are more likely to trust the system and engage with it positively.

Accessibility is another essential consideration in designing identity systems that balance security and user experience. Systems must be inclusive and usable by individuals with diverse abilities and needs. For example, biometric authentication methods should accommodate users with disabilities that affect fingerprint recognition or facial scanning. Similarly, MFA methods should offer alternatives for users who may not have access to mobile devices or who experience difficulties with certain technologies. Ensuring that identity systems are accessible not only broadens their usability but also aligns with legal and ethical standards for inclusivity.

The integration of artificial intelligence (AI) and machine learning (ML) into identity systems offers new opportunities to balance security and user experience. AI-driven systems can analyze user behavior and detect anomalies in real time, enabling proactive security measures without intrusive prompts. For example, if a user's login behavior suddenly changes—such as logging in from a new location or at an unusual time—the system can flag the activity and request additional verification. Conversely, if the behavior aligns with established patterns, the system can streamline access. This context-aware approach minimizes unnecessary friction while maintaining strong security.

Regular user feedback and continuous improvement are essential for maintaining the balance between security and user experience. Organizations should actively seek input from users about their experiences with identity systems, identifying pain points and areas for enhancement. This feedback can inform iterative improvements to UI design, authentication processes, and support services. Additionally, conducting usability testing with diverse user groups can reveal insights into how different populations interact with the system and what adjustments are needed to optimize both security and convenience.

Ultimately, balancing user experience and security in identity systems requires a holistic, user-centered approach. It involves not only implementing robust technical measures but also understanding user behaviors, expectations, and needs. By adopting flexible, adaptive security models, prioritizing intuitive design, and fostering transparency and control, organizations can create identity systems that protect sensitive information while offering seamless, engaging experiences for users. As technology continues to evolve and the threat landscape shifts, maintaining this balance will be crucial for building trust, ensuring compliance, and supporting the growing demands of the digital world.

Common Pitfalls in Identity Authentication and How to Avoid Them

Identity authentication is the cornerstone of modern cybersecurity, ensuring that only authorized individuals can access sensitive information and systems. Despite advances in technology and widespread awareness of security threats, many organizations continue to fall into common pitfalls that compromise the effectiveness of their authentication processes. These mistakes not only expose systems to unauthorized access but also create vulnerabilities that can be exploited by cybercriminals. Understanding these pitfalls and adopting best practices to avoid them is essential for maintaining robust security and protecting user data.

One of the most prevalent pitfalls in identity authentication is the over-reliance on passwords as the primary form of security. While passwords have been a foundational element of authentication for decades, they are inherently vulnerable to a range of attacks, including phishing, brute force attacks, and credential stuffing. Users often contribute to this vulnerability by choosing weak, easily guessable passwords or reusing the same password across multiple accounts. This behavior significantly increases the risk of account compromise, especially in the event of a data breach where stolen credentials can be leveraged across different platforms.

To mitigate the risks associated with passwords, organizations should implement multi-factor authentication (MFA). MFA requires users to provide two or more forms of verification, such as a password combined with a one-time code sent to a mobile device or biometric authentication like a fingerprint scan. This additional layer of security makes it much more difficult for attackers to gain unauthorized access, even if they have obtained a user's password. However, it's important to ensure that the MFA process itself is user-friendly and accessible, as overly complicated systems can lead to frustration and reduce adoption rates.

Another common pitfall is poor password management practices within organizations. This includes failing to enforce strong password policies, neglecting to educate users about secure password creation, and not providing tools to help manage complex credentials. Password policies should require a mix of uppercase and lowercase letters, numbers, and special characters, and discourage the use of common words or easily guessable information like birthdates. Regularly prompting users to change their passwords can also help mitigate risks, though this should be balanced to avoid unnecessary inconvenience that might lead users to adopt insecure habits, like writing passwords down.

Inadequate handling of password resets is another frequent issue. Many systems rely on easily exploitable security questions for password recovery, such as "What is your mother's maiden name?" or "What was the name of your first pet?" The answers to these questions are often easily obtainable through social media or other public sources, rendering them ineffective as security measures. To improve the security of password recovery processes, organizations should use more robust verification methods, such as sending reset links to verified email addresses or using secondary authentication factors.

Storing passwords in an insecure manner is a critical pitfall that can have devastating consequences if a system is breached. Some organizations still store passwords in plaintext or use outdated, weak hashing algorithms that can be easily cracked. Best practices dictate that passwords should always be hashed and salted using strong, modern cryptographic algorithms like bcrypt or Argon2. Salting adds a unique value to each password before hashing, ensuring that even identical passwords result in different hash values, which protects against rainbow table attacks.

Phishing attacks remain one of the most effective methods for compromising user credentials, yet many organizations fail to adequately protect against them. Phishing involves tricking users into providing their login information by masquerading as a trustworthy entity, often through emails or fake websites. To combat phishing, organizations should implement email filtering systems to detect and block phishing attempts, provide regular training to employees on how to recognize phishing emails, and encourage the use of MFA to add an extra layer of protection. Advanced phishing-resistant authentication methods, such as hardware security keys that comply with FIDO2 standards, can also provide robust defense against these attacks.

Another significant pitfall in identity authentication is failing to account for insider threats. While much focus is placed on external attackers, employees or other trusted individuals with legitimate access can also pose risks, either through malicious intent or negligence. Organizations should implement strict access controls, ensuring that users only have access to the information necessary for their role. Regular audits and monitoring of access logs can help detect unusual behavior that might indicate an insider threat. Additionally, fostering a culture of security awareness within the organization can reduce the likelihood of negligent behavior leading to security breaches.

Neglecting to update and patch authentication systems is another common oversight that can lead to vulnerabilities. Software and hardware used in authentication processes often receive updates that address newly discovered security flaws. Failing to apply these updates promptly can leave systems exposed to exploitation. Organizations should establish regular update and patch management processes to ensure that all authentication-related software and hardware are kept up-to-date with the latest security enhancements.

Another pitfall is the improper implementation of Single Sign-On (SSO) solutions. While SSO can greatly enhance user convenience by allowing access to multiple systems with a single login, it also creates a single point of failure if not properly secured. If an attacker compromises the SSO credentials, they may gain access to all connected systems. To mitigate this risk, organizations should implement strong MFA for SSO logins, regularly review and audit access permissions, and ensure that the SSO provider follows best practices in security.

Failing to consider the user experience in authentication design can also lead to security issues. If authentication processes are too cumbersome or intrusive, users may seek ways to circumvent them, such as disabling security features or using insecure methods to store credentials. Balancing security with usability is crucial. This can be achieved by adopting user-friendly authentication methods like biometrics or adaptive authentication, which adjusts security requirements based on the context of the login attempt, such as location or device.

Lastly, a common pitfall is the lack of continuous monitoring and improvement of authentication systems. Cyber threats evolve rapidly, and static security measures quickly become outdated. Organizations should adopt a proactive approach to identity authentication, continuously monitoring for new threats, assessing the effectiveness of current security measures, and adapting to emerging technologies and best practices. Regular security assessments, penetration testing, and red team exercises can help identify weaknesses in authentication systems before they can be exploited by attackers.

By understanding and addressing these common pitfalls in identity authentication, organizations can significantly enhance their security posture and protect against unauthorized access and data breaches. Implementing strong, multi-layered authentication processes, fostering a culture of security awareness, and continuously adapting to evolving threats are key strategies for maintaining robust identity security in an increasingly digital world.

Disaster Recovery and Business Continuity for Identity Systems

In today's digitally interconnected world, identity systems are the backbone of secure access to applications, data, and networks. They govern who can access what resources, ensuring that only authorized individuals can interact with sensitive information. Given their critical role, any disruption to identity systems—whether due to cyberattacks, natural disasters, technical failures, or human errors—can have far-reaching consequences. Such disruptions not only compromise security but can also halt business operations, erode customer trust, and lead to financial losses. Therefore, robust disaster recovery (DR) and business continuity (BC) strategies are essential to maintain the availability, integrity, and resilience of identity systems in the face of unexpected events.

Disaster recovery focuses on the restoration of IT infrastructure and data following a disruptive incident, ensuring that critical systems, such as identity management platforms, are brought back online as quickly as possible. Business continuity, on the other hand, is a broader strategy that ensures essential business functions can continue during and after a disaster, minimizing downtime and operational disruption. Together, these strategies create a comprehensive framework that prepares organizations to respond to and recover from various types of incidents, safeguarding the integrity and availability of their identity systems.

One of the first steps in developing a disaster recovery and business continuity plan for identity systems is conducting a thorough risk assessment. This involves identifying potential threats that could impact identity infrastructure, such as cyberattacks, power outages, hardware failures, natural disasters, and insider threats. Understanding the likelihood and potential impact of these threats allows organizations to prioritize their resources and focus on the most critical vulnerabilities. For instance, in regions prone to natural disasters like earthquakes or hurricanes, physical data center resilience becomes a priority, while in industries frequently targeted by cybercriminals, such as finance or healthcare, strengthening cybersecurity defenses is essential.

Once risks are identified, organizations should perform a business impact analysis (BIA) to determine the potential consequences of identity system disruptions. The BIA assesses how long the organization can tolerate downtime before experiencing significant operational, financial, or reputational damage. Two key metrics emerge from this analysis: the Recovery Time Objective (RTO) and the Recovery Point Objective (RPO). RTO defines the maximum acceptable downtime before the identity system must be restored, while RPO specifies the maximum amount of data loss that is tolerable, typically measured in minutes or hours. These metrics guide the design of disaster recovery solutions, ensuring that they meet the organization's specific resilience requirements.

Redundancy and failover mechanisms are critical components of disaster recovery for identity systems. Redundancy involves creating duplicate instances of identity infrastructure components, such as authentication servers, directory services, and databases, which can take over in case of a failure. Failover mechanisms automatically switch to these redundant systems when a primary system becomes unavailable, ensuring continuous access to identity services with minimal interruption. For example, deploying identity systems across multiple geographically dispersed data centers or cloud regions helps protect against localized disasters, allowing traffic to be rerouted to unaffected sites.

Cloud-based identity solutions offer inherent advantages for disaster recovery and business continuity. Many organizations are migrating their identity infrastructure to cloud providers like Microsoft Azure Active Directory, Amazon Web Services (AWS) Identity and Access Management (IAM), or Google Cloud Identity. These platforms provide built-in redundancy, scalability, and high availability, reducing the complexity and cost of maintaining on-premises disaster recovery environments. Additionally, cloud providers often offer service-level agreements (SLAs) that guarantee uptime and data durability, providing organizations with confidence in the resilience of their identity systems.

Data backup is another fundamental aspect of disaster recovery for identity systems. Regular, automated backups of identity data— including user accounts, authentication credentials, access control lists, and configuration settings—are essential to ensure that information can be restored in the event of data corruption, accidental deletion, or ransomware attacks. Backups should be stored in secure, offsite locations, preferably in multiple geographic regions, to protect against localized disasters. It is also crucial to regularly test backup and restoration processes to ensure that data can be recovered quickly and accurately when needed.

Access control during and after a disaster is a critical consideration for business continuity. In the chaos of a disruptive event, it is essential to maintain strict control over who can access identity systems and recovery tools. Implementing role-based access control (RBAC) ensures that only authorized personnel have the necessary permissions to execute recovery procedures. Additionally, multi-factor authentication (MFA) should be enforced for all administrative accounts to prevent unauthorized access, even in the event of credential compromise. Emergency access protocols, sometimes referred to as "break-glass" procedures, should be established to allow designated individuals to bypass certain security measures in critical situations while ensuring that these actions are thoroughly logged and audited.

Communication is a vital element of business continuity planning for identity systems. Clear communication protocols should be established to inform employees, stakeholders, and customers about the status of identity systems during a disruption. This includes notifying users of service outages, providing guidance on accessing alternative resources, and updating them on the progress of recovery efforts. Internally, IT and security teams must coordinate closely, sharing information about the nature of the incident, the status of recovery operations, and any emerging threats. Communication plans should include predefined templates and contact lists to streamline information dissemination during high-pressure situations.

Regular testing and simulation exercises are essential to ensure the effectiveness of disaster recovery and business continuity plans for identity systems. Organizations should conduct periodic drills, such as tabletop exercises and full-scale simulations, to validate their recovery procedures and identify areas for improvement. These exercises help familiarize staff with their roles and responsibilities during a disaster, uncover gaps in the plan, and ensure that recovery time objectives can be met. Testing also provides an opportunity to evaluate the performance of failover systems, backup processes, and communication protocols in real-world scenarios.

Continuous monitoring and incident detection play a critical role in both disaster recovery and business continuity for identity systems. Implementing robust monitoring tools that provide real-time visibility into the health and performance of identity infrastructure allows organizations to detect issues early and respond proactively. Security Information and Event Management (SIEM) systems can aggregate and analyze logs from identity systems, helping identify potential security incidents, such as unauthorized access attempts or unusual login patterns. Integrating identity monitoring with broader cybersecurity tools enhances situational awareness and supports a coordinated response to incidents.

Documentation is another key component of an effective disaster recovery and business continuity strategy. Detailed, up-to-date documentation should outline every aspect of the recovery process, including step-by-step procedures, configuration settings, contact information for key personnel, and escalation paths. This documentation should be easily accessible, both online and offline, to ensure that it can be referenced during a crisis. Regularly reviewing and updating documentation ensures that it reflects the current state of identity systems and incorporates lessons learned from previous incidents and tests.

Vendor and third-party management is an often-overlooked aspect of disaster recovery for identity systems. Many organizations rely on third-party services and software for their identity infrastructure, such as identity-as-a-service (IDaaS) providers, cloud platforms, and authentication tools. It is essential to assess the disaster recovery capabilities of these vendors and ensure that they align with the organization's resilience requirements. Service-level agreements should clearly define expectations for uptime, data recovery, and incident response. Additionally, organizations should develop contingency plans for scenarios where third-party services become unavailable, including fallback procedures and alternative providers.

Finally, fostering a culture of resilience within the organization is crucial for the success of disaster recovery and business continuity efforts. This involves training employees on the importance of identity security, encouraging proactive risk management, and promoting collaboration across departments. Leadership should prioritize resilience as a strategic objective, allocating resources and support to maintain robust identity systems and recovery processes. By embedding resilience into the organization's culture, businesses can better withstand disruptions and emerge stronger from crises.

In the ever-evolving threat landscape, disaster recovery and business continuity planning for identity systems are not optional—they are essential components of a comprehensive cybersecurity strategy. By anticipating potential risks, implementing robust recovery mechanisms, and fostering a culture of preparedness, organizations can ensure the resilience and integrity of their identity systems, protecting both their operations and their reputation in the face of adversity.

Third-Party Access: Managing External Identities

In today's interconnected digital ecosystem, organizations increasingly rely on third-party vendors, contractors, partners, and suppliers to deliver products and services, streamline operations, and foster innovation. While these external entities play a critical role in business growth and efficiency, granting them access to internal systems, data, and applications introduces significant security risks. Managing third-party access, often referred to as managing external identities, has become a vital component of modern identity and access management (IAM). Without proper controls, third-party access can become a weak link in an organization's security posture, potentially leading to data breaches, compliance violations, and reputational damage.

The complexity of managing external identities stems from the diverse nature of third-party relationships. Unlike internal employees, third-party users often have varying roles, access needs, and contractual obligations. Some may require temporary access to specific systems, while others may need ongoing access to critical infrastructure.

Additionally, third-party users may not be subject to the same security training, policies, or oversight as internal staff, increasing the likelihood of accidental or intentional security breaches. Therefore, organizations must implement robust, flexible, and scalable IAM frameworks to manage these external identities effectively.

One of the foundational principles of managing third-party access is the concept of least privilege. This principle dictates that users— whether internal or external—should have the minimum level of access necessary to perform their job functions. For third-party users, this means granting access only to the specific systems, applications, or data required for their role, and nothing more. Implementing role-based access control (RBAC) is an effective way to enforce this principle. RBAC assigns permissions based on predefined roles within the organization, ensuring that third-party users can only access resources relevant to their contractual responsibilities. By limiting access to what is strictly necessary, organizations reduce the risk of unauthorized data exposure and potential security breaches.

In addition to RBAC, organizations should adopt attribute-based access control (ABAC) to manage more granular and dynamic access requirements. ABAC evaluates a combination of attributes, such as user identity, role, location, and time of access, to determine permissions. For example, a contractor might be granted access to a specific database only during business hours and only from a verified corporate device. ABAC provides a flexible framework for managing third-party access, allowing organizations to adapt permissions based on contextual factors and evolving security needs.

Identity federation is another key strategy for managing external identities. Federation allows organizations to establish trust relationships with third-party identity providers (IdPs), enabling seamless and secure authentication across organizational boundaries. Through standardized protocols like SAML (Security Assertion Markup Language) and OpenID Connect, third-party users can authenticate using their existing credentials from their home organization, reducing the need for managing separate accounts and passwords. Federation not only simplifies the user experience but also enhances security by leveraging the authentication mechanisms and security policies of trusted partners.

While federation facilitates secure authentication, organizations must also implement stringent verification processes before granting access to third-party users. This includes conducting thorough due diligence on third-party entities to assess their security practices, compliance with relevant regulations, and overall trustworthiness. Vendor risk assessments should evaluate factors such as data handling procedures, cybersecurity protocols, and incident response capabilities. Establishing clear contractual agreements that outline security requirements, access protocols, and compliance obligations is essential to ensure that third parties adhere to the organization's security standards.

Multi-factor authentication (MFA) is a critical security measure for managing third-party access. By requiring multiple forms of verification—such as a password combined with a one-time code sent to a mobile device or biometric authentication—MFA significantly reduces the risk of unauthorized access, even if a third party's credentials are compromised. Organizations should enforce MFA for all third-party users, particularly those accessing sensitive systems or data. Additionally, adaptive authentication can be employed to adjust security requirements based on the risk level of the access attempt, providing a balance between security and user convenience.

Provisioning and de-provisioning are crucial aspects of managing external identities. Organizations must establish automated processes for granting, modifying, and revoking third-party access in a timely and efficient manner. When a third-party relationship begins, access should be provisioned based on predefined roles and attributes, ensuring that users have the appropriate permissions from the outset. Equally important is the de-provisioning process, which ensures that access is promptly revoked when a third-party contract ends, a project is completed, or a user's role changes. Failure to properly de-provision accounts can lead to orphaned accounts—unused accounts that remain active and can be exploited by malicious actors.

Monitoring and auditing third-party access is essential for maintaining security and compliance. Organizations should implement continuous monitoring tools to track third-party activities, detect anomalies, and respond to potential security incidents. Security Information and Event Management (SIEM) systems can aggregate logs from various sources, providing real-time visibility into third-party access patterns and behaviors. Regular audits and access reviews help ensure that permissions remain appropriate and that any deviations from established security policies are promptly addressed. These audits are also critical for demonstrating compliance with regulatory requirements such as GDPR, HIPAA, and SOX, which mandate strict controls over third-party access to sensitive data.

Communication and collaboration between organizations and their third-party partners are vital for effective identity management. Clear communication protocols should be established to address security incidents, changes in access requirements, and updates to security policies. Regular meetings and security briefings can help align expectations and ensure that third-party users are aware of their responsibilities regarding data protection and cybersecurity. In the event of a security breach involving a third party, coordinated incident response plans are essential for mitigating the impact and restoring normal operations.

The use of dedicated third-party identity management platforms can further enhance the security and efficiency of managing external identities. These platforms provide centralized tools for onboarding, authenticating, and monitoring third-party users, integrating seamlessly with existing IAM systems. Features such as self-service portals, automated workflows, and detailed reporting capabilities streamline the management of third-party access, reducing administrative overhead and improving security posture. By leveraging specialized solutions, organizations can gain greater control over external identities and ensure consistent enforcement of security policies.

Emerging technologies such as blockchain and decentralized identity (DID) frameworks offer innovative approaches to managing third-party identities. Blockchain technology provides a secure, immutable ledger for recording identity transactions, enhancing transparency and trust between organizations and their third-party partners. Decentralized identity systems enable users to own and control their identity data, sharing only the necessary information with organizations for authentication purposes. This approach reduces the risk of data breaches by minimizing the amount of personal information stored in centralized databases and enhances privacy for third-party users.

As the digital landscape continues to evolve, the importance of managing third-party access will only grow. The increasing reliance on cloud services, remote work, and global supply chains expands the network of external entities interacting with organizational systems, creating new challenges and opportunities for identity management. Organizations must stay proactive in adapting their IAM strategies to address these changes, leveraging advanced technologies, best practices, and continuous improvement to safeguard their systems and data.

Ultimately, effective management of third-party access requires a holistic approach that integrates technology, policy, and human factors. By implementing robust authentication mechanisms, enforcing strict access controls, conducting regular audits, and fostering strong partnerships with third-party entities, organizations can mitigate the risks associated with external identities and ensure the security and integrity of their digital ecosystems. In doing so, they can build resilient, trustworthy relationships with their partners, driving business growth while maintaining a strong security posture in an increasingly interconnected world.

Cross-Border Identity Challenges in a Globalized World

In an increasingly interconnected world, the movement of people, goods, and information across national borders has become a defining characteristic of globalization. This global exchange offers immense opportunities for economic growth, cultural exchange, and technological advancement. However, it also presents complex challenges, particularly in the realm of identity management. As individuals and organizations interact across different jurisdictions, the need for secure, interoperable, and trustworthy identity systems becomes paramount. Cross-border identity management involves ensuring that digital identities are authenticated, authorized, and managed in a way that respects national regulations, cultural differences, and the diverse technological landscapes of various countries.

One of the primary challenges in cross-border identity management is the lack of standardized frameworks and protocols for verifying identities across different jurisdictions. While many countries have developed robust national identity systems, these systems often operate in isolation, using unique standards, technologies, and legal frameworks. For example, the European Union's eIDAS (Electronic Identification, Authentication, and Trust Services) regulation establishes a standardized framework for electronic identification within the EU, but its applicability and interoperability with systems outside the EU remain limited. Similarly, other regions and countries may have their own digital identity solutions that do not easily integrate with international counterparts. This fragmentation complicates efforts to create seamless cross-border identity verification processes.

The diversity of legal and regulatory requirements across countries further complicates cross-border identity management. Different jurisdictions have varying standards for data protection, privacy, and identity verification, making it difficult to establish a unified approach. For instance, the European Union's General Data Protection Regulation (GDPR) imposes stringent requirements on data privacy and the handling of personal information, while other countries may have less comprehensive or entirely different data protection laws. Organizations operating internationally must navigate these complex legal landscapes, ensuring that their identity management practices comply with all relevant regulations. This often involves balancing conflicting requirements and adapting systems to meet diverse legal standards.

Data sovereignty is another critical issue in cross-border identity management. Many countries have enacted laws that require personal data to be stored and processed within their national borders, limiting the ability of organizations to centralize identity data in global data centers. This can create significant challenges for multinational corporations that seek to implement unified identity systems across their global operations. Ensuring compliance with data sovereignty laws often requires developing localized identity solutions, which can increase complexity and cost while reducing the efficiency of global operations.

Cultural differences and varying levels of technological infrastructure also play a role in cross-border identity challenges. In some countries, biometric authentication methods such as fingerprint scanning or facial recognition are widely accepted and integrated into daily life, while in others, there may be cultural resistance or legal restrictions on the use of such technologies. Additionally, the availability and reliability of internet access and digital infrastructure can vary significantly between countries, affecting the feasibility of certain identity management solutions. Organizations must consider these factors when designing identity systems for international use, ensuring that their solutions are adaptable and sensitive to local contexts.

Interoperability is a key objective in addressing cross-border identity challenges. Achieving interoperability requires the development and adoption of international standards and protocols that facilitate secure and seamless identity verification across different systems and jurisdictions. Initiatives such as the International Organization for Standardization (ISO) standards for identity management and the efforts of organizations like the OpenID Foundation aim to create common frameworks for digital identity that can be used globally. However, achieving widespread adoption of these standards requires collaboration among governments, industry stakeholders, and technology providers, as well as ongoing efforts to address the technical, legal, and cultural barriers to interoperability.

Federated identity management is one approach to facilitating cross-border identity verification. Federation allows multiple organizations or entities to share and trust each other's identity verification processes, enabling users to authenticate once and access services across different jurisdictions. For example, a user who authenticates with their national identity provider could access services in another country that participates in the same federation framework. While federated identity systems offer a promising solution, they also require robust trust frameworks, clear governance structures, and agreements on security and privacy standards to ensure their effectiveness and reliability.

Blockchain and decentralized identity (DID) technologies are emerging as innovative solutions to cross-border identity challenges. Decentralized identity systems enable individuals to own and control their digital identities, using cryptographic proofs to verify their credentials without relying on centralized authorities. This approach enhances privacy and security while facilitating cross-border interactions by allowing users to share only the necessary information for specific transactions. Blockchain technology provides a secure and immutable ledger for recording identity transactions, ensuring transparency and trust in cross-border identity verification processes. However, the widespread adoption of these technologies faces challenges related to scalability, regulatory acceptance, and technical standardization.

Cross-border identity management is particularly critical in sectors such as finance, healthcare, and travel, where secure and efficient identity verification is essential for compliance, safety, and operational efficiency. In the financial sector, for example, institutions must comply with anti-money laundering (AML) and know-your-customer (KYC) regulations, which require robust identity verification processes for international transactions. Ensuring that these processes are consistent and reliable across different jurisdictions is essential for preventing fraud, money laundering, and other financial crimes. Similarly, in healthcare, cross-border identity management enables the secure sharing of medical records and patient information, facilitating international collaboration in research and treatment while protecting patient privacy.

The rise of remote work and the global gig economy has further highlighted the importance of cross-border identity management. Organizations increasingly hire employees, contractors, and freelancers from around the world, necessitating secure and efficient identity verification processes for onboarding, access management, and compliance. Ensuring that these processes are consistent and scalable across different countries and regulatory environments is essential for maintaining security and operational efficiency in a globally distributed workforce.

Government-led initiatives and international collaborations are playing a significant role in addressing cross-border identity challenges. The European Union's eIDAS regulation, for example, aims to create a unified framework for electronic identification and trust services across EU member states, facilitating secure cross-border digital interactions. Similarly, initiatives such as the United Nations' efforts to establish digital identity frameworks for global development and the World Bank's ID4D (Identification for Development) program aim to promote inclusive, secure, and interoperable identity systems worldwide. These initiatives highlight the importance of cross-border collaboration in developing effective identity management solutions that can address the challenges of globalization.

As the digital landscape continues to evolve, the need for robust and interoperable cross-border identity management systems will only grow. Organizations must stay proactive in adapting their identity management strategies to meet the demands of a globalized world, leveraging emerging technologies, international standards, and collaborative efforts to create secure and seamless identity verification processes. By addressing the legal, technical, and cultural challenges associated with cross-border identity management, organizations can enhance security, facilitate international collaboration, and support the continued growth and innovation of the global digital economy.

The Role of Identity in Digital Transformation Initiatives

In the rapidly evolving landscape of the modern business world, digital transformation has become a cornerstone for organizations seeking to remain competitive, agile, and innovative. Digital transformation refers to the integration of digital technologies into all areas of a business, fundamentally changing how organizations operate and deliver value to customers. At the heart of these initiatives lies identity management, a critical enabler of secure, efficient, and personalized digital experiences. The ability to accurately authenticate, authorize, and manage the identities of users, devices, and applications is essential for realizing the full potential of digital transformation.

Identity plays a pivotal role in digital transformation by ensuring secure access to digital resources and fostering trust between users and organizations. As businesses move to cloud-based infrastructures, adopt remote work models, and embrace new digital services, the traditional perimeter-based security model becomes obsolete. Instead, organizations must adopt identity-centric security frameworks, where access to systems and data is governed by the verified identities of users and devices, regardless of their location or network. This shift places identity and access management (IAM) at the forefront of digital transformation strategies.

One of the primary drivers of digital transformation is the move to cloud computing. Cloud platforms offer scalability, flexibility, and cost-efficiency, enabling organizations to rapidly deploy and manage applications and services. However, this transition also introduces new security challenges, as sensitive data and critical applications are no longer confined to on-premises environments. Effective identity management is essential for securing cloud environments, ensuring that only authorized users can access cloud resources. This involves implementing robust authentication mechanisms, such as multi-factor authentication (MFA), and leveraging federated identity systems that allow seamless access across multiple cloud platforms and services.

The rise of remote work and the global workforce has further underscored the importance of identity in digital transformation. With employees accessing corporate systems from various locations and devices, organizations must ensure that their identity management systems can support secure and flexible access. This includes enabling single sign-on (SSO) capabilities that allow users to authenticate once and access multiple applications without repeatedly entering credentials. Additionally, identity management solutions must be able to adapt to the dynamic nature of remote work, providing context-aware access controls that consider factors such as device type, location, and user behavior.

Personalization is another key aspect of digital transformation, and identity management plays a crucial role in delivering tailored experiences to users. By leveraging identity data, organizations can gain insights into user preferences, behaviors, and needs, enabling them to offer personalized products, services, and interactions. For example, e-commerce platforms can use identity data to recommend products based on a user's browsing history and purchase behavior, while financial institutions can tailor investment advice to individual customer profiles. Effective identity management ensures that this personalization is both accurate and secure, protecting user privacy while enhancing the customer experience.

In addition to enhancing security and personalization, identity management supports operational efficiency in digital transformation initiatives. Automating identity-related processes, such as user provisioning, de-provisioning, and access reviews, reduces administrative overhead and minimizes the risk of human error. Role-based access control (RBAC) and attribute-based access control (ABAC) frameworks streamline the assignment of permissions, ensuring that users have the appropriate access rights based on their roles and responsibilities. This not only improves security but also enables faster onboarding and offboarding, enhancing overall productivity.

As organizations adopt digital transformation initiatives, they must also navigate complex regulatory landscapes that govern data protection and privacy. Regulations such as the General Data Protection Regulation (GDPR) and the California Consumer Privacy Act (CCPA) impose strict requirements on how personal data is collected, stored, and processed. Identity management systems play a critical role in ensuring compliance with these regulations by providing tools for data governance, consent management, and audit logging. By maintaining detailed records of user access and activity, organizations can demonstrate compliance with regulatory requirements and respond effectively to audits and data subject requests.

The integration of emerging technologies into digital transformation initiatives further highlights the importance of identity management. Artificial intelligence (AI) and machine learning (ML) are increasingly being used to enhance identity verification and threat detection processes. AI-driven systems can analyze patterns of user behavior to identify anomalies that may indicate security threats, such as unauthorized access attempts or credential theft. Machine learning algorithms can continuously adapt to new threats, improving the accuracy and effectiveness of identity management solutions over time. By leveraging these technologies, organizations can enhance both security and user experience in their digital transformation efforts.

Blockchain technology also offers innovative approaches to identity management in digital transformation. Decentralized identity frameworks, which use blockchain to provide secure and verifiable digital identities, enable individuals to control their own identity data and share it selectively with organizations. This approach enhances privacy and security while reducing the risk of data breaches and identity theft. Blockchain-based identity solutions can also streamline cross-border transactions and interactions, facilitating seamless digital experiences in a globalized world.

Identity management is not only about securing access to digital resources but also about fostering trust in digital interactions. Trust is a fundamental component of digital transformation, as users must feel confident that their personal information is protected and that their digital interactions are secure. Transparent and user-centric identity management practices, such as providing clear privacy policies, offering control over personal data, and ensuring secure authentication processes, help build and maintain this trust. Organizations that prioritize trust in their digital transformation strategies are better positioned to attract and retain customers, employees, and partners.

The role of identity in digital transformation extends beyond individual organizations to encompass broader ecosystems and partnerships. As businesses collaborate with external partners, suppliers, and third-party service providers, managing external identities becomes critical for ensuring secure and efficient interactions. Federated identity systems and identity federation protocols, such as SAML and OpenID Connect, enable secure and seamless access across organizational boundaries. By establishing trust frameworks and governance structures, organizations can manage external identities effectively, supporting collaboration and innovation in digital ecosystems.

Identity management also plays a crucial role in enabling digital transformation in specific industries. In healthcare, for example, secure identity management is essential for protecting patient data and enabling secure access to electronic health records (EHRs). Digital transformation initiatives in healthcare, such as telemedicine and health information exchanges, rely on robust identity verification processes to ensure patient privacy and data security. Similarly, in the financial sector, identity management is critical for complying with regulatory requirements, preventing fraud, and delivering personalized financial services.

As digital transformation initiatives continue to evolve, organizations must adopt a strategic approach to identity management that aligns with their broader business goals and objectives. This involves investing in modern IAM solutions that support scalability, flexibility, and interoperability, as well as fostering a culture of security and privacy awareness. Continuous improvement and adaptation are essential, as the digital landscape and threat environment are constantly changing.

Ultimately, identity management is a foundational element of digital transformation, enabling organizations to secure access to digital resources, deliver personalized experiences, ensure regulatory compliance, and foster trust in digital interactions. By prioritizing identity management in their digital transformation strategies, organizations can unlock new opportunities for innovation, efficiency, and growth, positioning themselves for success in an increasingly digital world.

Identity Management for Remote Workforces

The rapid shift toward remote work, accelerated by global events and technological advancements, has transformed how organizations operate and manage their workforces. As businesses adapt to distributed teams and virtual collaboration, the role of identity management has become increasingly critical. In a traditional office environment, security relied heavily on perimeter-based defenses, where physical access to corporate networks was restricted and monitored. However, in a remote work model, the perimeter dissolves, and identity becomes the new cornerstone of security. Ensuring that the right individuals have access to the right resources, at the right time, from any location, is essential for maintaining productivity, protecting sensitive data, and mitigating security risks.

Identity management for remote workforces involves authenticating users, managing their access to digital resources, and ensuring secure interactions across diverse locations and devices. This shift presents unique challenges, as remote employees connect from home networks, public Wi-Fi, and personal devices, often outside the direct control of the organization's IT infrastructure. Without proper identity management practices, organizations risk unauthorized access, data breaches, and compliance violations.

One of the foundational elements of identity management for remote workforces is robust authentication. Passwords, long the standard for securing user accounts, are no longer sufficient in the remote work era. Passwords can be easily stolen, guessed, or phished, especially when employees are working outside the protective environment of a corporate network. Multi-factor authentication (MFA) has become a critical tool for strengthening security. MFA requires users to provide two or more forms of verification—such as a password combined with a one-time code sent to a mobile device, or biometric authentication like a fingerprint scan. By adding additional layers of verification, MFA significantly reduces the risk of unauthorized access, even if a password is compromised.

While MFA enhances security, it must also be implemented in a way that balances user convenience with protection. Overly complex or intrusive authentication processes can frustrate employees and hinder productivity. Adaptive authentication offers a solution by adjusting security requirements based on contextual factors, such as the user's location, device, and behavior. For example, if an employee logs in from a recognized device and location, the system might require only a single authentication factor, while an unfamiliar login attempt from a new device or country would trigger full MFA. This dynamic approach provides strong security while minimizing disruptions to the user experience.

Single sign-on (SSO) is another critical component of identity management for remote workforces. SSO allows employees to authenticate once and gain access to multiple applications and services without repeatedly entering credentials. This simplifies the login process, reduces the risk of password fatigue, and minimizes the likelihood of insecure practices such as writing down passwords or reusing them across different platforms. From an IT perspective, SSO centralizes authentication, enabling more consistent enforcement of security policies and easier monitoring of access activities.

The rise of cloud-based applications and services has further complicated identity management for remote workforces. Many organizations rely on a mix of on-premises systems, cloud platforms, and third-party applications, each with its own authentication mechanisms and access controls. Federated identity management provides a solution by establishing trust relationships between different identity providers, allowing users to access multiple systems with a single set of credentials. Protocols such as SAML (Security Assertion Markup Language) and OpenID Connect facilitate this interoperability, enabling seamless and secure access across diverse environments.

Device management is another crucial aspect of identity management in remote work settings. Employees often use personal devices to access corporate resources, a practice known as Bring Your Own Device (BYOD). While BYOD offers flexibility and convenience, it also introduces security risks, as personal devices may lack the security controls and monitoring capabilities of corporate-issued hardware. Mobile device management (MDM) and endpoint detection and response (EDR) solutions help mitigate these risks by enforcing security policies, monitoring device activity, and enabling remote wiping of data in case of loss or theft. Integrating device management with identity systems ensures that access is granted only from secure, compliant devices.

Access control is a fundamental principle of identity management, and it becomes even more critical in a remote work environment. Role-based access control (RBAC) and attribute-based access control (ABAC) frameworks help ensure that employees have access only to the resources necessary for their roles. RBAC assigns permissions based on predefined roles within the organization, while ABAC evaluates a combination of attributes, such as user identity, device, location, and time of access, to determine permissions. By implementing granular access controls, organizations can minimize the risk of unauthorized data exposure and limit the potential impact of security breaches.

Continuous monitoring and auditing of user activities are essential for maintaining security in a remote workforce. Security Information and Event Management (SIEM) systems aggregate and analyze logs from various sources, providing real-time visibility into user behavior and detecting anomalies that may indicate security threats. For example, if an employee's account shows an unusual pattern of access, such as logging in from multiple locations simultaneously or accessing sensitive data outside normal working hours, the system can trigger alerts for further investigation. Regular audits and access reviews help ensure that permissions remain appropriate and that any deviations from established security policies are promptly addressed.

The shift to remote work also brings new challenges related to compliance with data protection regulations. Laws such as the General Data Protection Regulation (GDPR) and the California Consumer Privacy Act (CCPA) impose strict requirements on how personal data is collected, stored, and processed. Identity management systems play a critical role in ensuring compliance by providing tools for data governance, consent management, and audit logging. By maintaining detailed records of user access and activity, organizations can demonstrate compliance with regulatory requirements and respond effectively to audits and data subject requests.

User education and awareness are vital components of a successful identity management strategy for remote workforces. Employees must be trained to recognize and respond to common security threats, such as phishing attacks, social engineering, and credential theft. Regular security awareness programs, simulated phishing exercises, and clear communication about best practices help foster a culture of security within the organization. When employees understand the importance of secure identity practices and feel empowered to take responsibility for their digital behavior, the overall security posture of the organization is strengthened.

The integration of artificial intelligence (AI) and machine learning (ML) into identity management systems offers new opportunities for enhancing security in remote work environments. AI-driven analytics can monitor user behavior, detect anomalies, and predict potential security threats based on historical data and patterns. For example, machine learning algorithms can identify subtle deviations in login behavior that may indicate a compromised account, enabling proactive responses before a breach occurs. By continuously adapting to new threats, AI and ML enhance the effectiveness of identity management solutions and support a proactive approach to security.

As organizations continue to embrace remote work, the role of identity management will only become more central to their security and operational strategies. Investing in modern IAM solutions that support scalability, flexibility, and interoperability is essential for enabling secure and efficient remote work. Organizations must also adopt a holistic approach that integrates technology, policy, and human factors, ensuring that identity management practices align with broader business goals and security objectives.

In the future, the convergence of technologies such as blockchain, decentralized identity frameworks, and advanced biometrics may further transform identity management for remote workforces. These innovations have the potential to enhance security, streamline authentication processes, and give users greater control over their digital identities. By staying agile and proactive in their identity management strategies, organizations can support the evolving needs of their remote workforces, protect sensitive data, and maintain a strong security posture in an increasingly digital and distributed world.

The Cost of Poor Identity Management: Breaches and Beyond

In the digital era, where businesses increasingly rely on online platforms and cloud-based systems, identity management has become a cornerstone of cybersecurity and operational efficiency. Identity management refers to the processes and technologies used to authenticate and authorize individuals accessing digital resources, ensuring that the right people have the right access at the right time. When executed effectively, it provides a seamless user experience while safeguarding sensitive data. However, poor identity management can lead to significant consequences that extend far beyond simple inconvenience. The financial, operational, reputational, and legal costs of failing to properly manage identities can cripple organizations, leading to data breaches, regulatory penalties, loss of customer trust, and long-term damage to business viability.

One of the most immediate and damaging consequences of poor identity management is data breaches. Data breaches often result from weak authentication mechanisms, inadequate access controls, and insufficient monitoring of user activities. When identity management systems fail to verify and restrict access effectively, unauthorized individuals—whether malicious insiders or external attackers—can exploit vulnerabilities to gain access to sensitive information. These breaches can expose personal data, financial information, intellectual property, and other critical assets, causing extensive harm to both organizations and individuals.

The financial cost of data breaches is staggering. According to industry reports, the average cost of a data breach runs into millions of dollars, factoring in direct expenses such as investigation, remediation, notification of affected parties, and legal fees. Additionally, organizations often face indirect costs, including business disruption, loss of revenue, and increased insurance premiums. For example, in the case of the infamous Equifax breach, the failure to manage identities and vulnerabilities appropriately led to the exposure of sensitive information for over 147 million individuals. The breach resulted in a $700 million settlement with the Federal Trade Commission (FTC) and ongoing legal costs, not to mention the incalculable damage to Equifax's reputation.

Beyond the immediate financial implications, poor identity management can lead to regulatory penalties and legal liabilities. With stringent data protection laws such as the General Data Protection Regulation (GDPR) in the European Union and the California Consumer Privacy Act (CCPA) in the United States, organizations are required to implement robust security measures to protect personal data. Failure to comply with these regulations can result in substantial fines and legal actions. GDPR, for instance, allows for penalties of up to 4% of an organization's annual global turnover or €20 million, whichever is higher, for serious breaches of data protection requirements. Organizations that neglect identity management not only risk breaches but also face legal scrutiny and financial repercussions for failing to meet regulatory obligations.

The reputational damage resulting from poor identity management can be even more devastating than financial losses. Trust is a fundamental element of any business relationship, and customers expect organizations to protect their personal information and provide secure digital interactions. When a data breach occurs due to inadequate identity management, it erodes customer confidence and loyalty. This loss of trust can lead to customer attrition, decreased market share, and negative publicity that tarnishes the brand's image for years. Rebuilding trust after a breach is an arduous process, often requiring significant investments in public relations, customer outreach, and enhanced security measures to reassure stakeholders.

Operational disruptions are another critical cost associated with poor identity management. When identity systems are compromised or fail to function correctly, it can paralyze business operations. Employees may be unable to access essential systems, customers may be locked out of their accounts, and critical business processes may come to a halt. This downtime can result in lost productivity, missed business opportunities, and delayed project timelines. In industries such as healthcare, finance, and critical infrastructure, where timely access to information is crucial, identity management failures can have life-threatening consequences or trigger widespread economic impacts.

Insider threats represent another dimension of the risks associated with poor identity management. While external cyberattacks often garner headlines, many security breaches are perpetrated by individuals within the organization who have legitimate access to sensitive systems and data. Without proper identity governance, organizations may grant excessive or inappropriate access rights, fail to monitor user activities effectively, or neglect to revoke access when employees change roles or leave the company. This creates opportunities for malicious insiders to exploit their access for personal gain or for negligent insiders to inadvertently expose data through careless actions. Implementing robust identity management practices, such as role-based access control (RBAC) and regular access reviews, is essential for mitigating these risks.

The proliferation of third-party vendors and contractors in modern business ecosystems further complicates identity management. Organizations often grant external parties access to their systems and data to facilitate business operations, collaboration, and service delivery. However, failing to manage these external identities securely can introduce significant vulnerabilities. Third-party breaches, where attackers exploit weak security practices among vendors to gain access to an organization's systems, are increasingly common. The 2013 Target data breach, where attackers infiltrated the company's network through a compromised HVAC vendor's credentials, serves as a stark reminder of the risks associated with poorly managed third-party access.

Inadequate identity management also hampers organizational agility and innovation. As businesses undergo digital transformation and adopt new technologies, the ability to quickly and securely onboard users, integrate new applications, and manage access across diverse environments is critical for maintaining competitiveness. Poor identity management practices create bottlenecks, slow down digital initiatives, and limit the organization's ability to adapt to changing market conditions. Conversely, robust identity management enables seamless integration of new technologies, supports remote work, and enhances collaboration across distributed teams, driving innovation and business growth.

The human factor is another critical consideration in the costs of poor identity management. Employees often bypass cumbersome security processes if they perceive them as obstacles to productivity. Weak or overly complex identity systems can lead to insecure workarounds, such as sharing credentials, using unauthorized devices, or disabling security features. These behaviors increase the risk of security breaches and undermine the effectiveness of the organization's cybersecurity strategy. By designing user-friendly identity management systems that balance security with convenience, organizations can foster a culture of security awareness and compliance.

Addressing the costs of poor identity management requires a proactive and comprehensive approach. Organizations must invest in modern identity and access management (IAM) solutions that provide centralized control, automation, and visibility into user activities. Implementing multi-factor authentication, single sign-on (SSO), and adaptive authentication enhances security while improving the user experience. Regularly conducting access reviews, monitoring user behavior, and enforcing the principle of least privilege help prevent unauthorized access and reduce the risk of insider threats.

Training and awareness programs are also essential for mitigating the human risks associated with identity management. Employees should be educated on the importance of secure identity practices, such as recognizing phishing attempts, creating strong passwords, and adhering to access policies. By fostering a security-conscious culture, organizations can empower employees to act as the first line of defense against identity-related threats.

Furthermore, organizations must establish clear policies and procedures for managing third-party access, ensuring that vendors and contractors adhere to the same security standards as internal users. This includes conducting thorough risk assessments, establishing contractual security requirements, and continuously monitoring third-party activities to detect potential threats.

In the evolving threat landscape, the cost of poor identity management is not limited to immediate financial losses but extends to long-term operational, legal, and reputational consequences. By prioritizing identity management as a critical component of their cybersecurity and business strategies, organizations can protect their assets, maintain customer trust, and ensure sustainable growth in an increasingly digital world.

Building a Scalable Identity Architecture

As organizations grow and expand their digital presence, the need for a robust, flexible, and scalable identity architecture becomes increasingly critical. Identity architecture refers to the framework of technologies, processes, and policies that manage how users are authenticated, authorized, and granted access to resources within an organization. A scalable identity architecture ensures that as the number of users, devices, applications, and services grows, the system can handle increased demand without compromising security, performance, or user experience. Building such an architecture requires thoughtful planning, leveraging modern technologies, and aligning identity strategies with business goals.

At the heart of scalable identity architecture is the ability to handle a growing number of users and devices across diverse environments. In today's digital landscape, organizations are no longer confined to traditional on-premises systems. Instead, they operate in hybrid and multi-cloud environments, supporting remote workforces, mobile access, and global user bases. This complexity demands an identity architecture that can seamlessly integrate with various platforms and provide consistent, secure access across all digital touchpoints.

One of the foundational components of a scalable identity architecture is centralized identity management. Centralization simplifies the management of user identities, credentials, and access rights by consolidating these functions into a unified system. This approach not only reduces administrative overhead but also enhances security by providing a single point of control for monitoring and enforcing access policies. Centralized identity management platforms, such as Microsoft Azure Active Directory, Okta, and Ping Identity, offer cloud-based solutions that support scalability and integration with a wide range of applications and services.

Single sign-on (SSO) is a critical feature of scalable identity architecture, allowing users to authenticate once and gain access to multiple applications without needing to re-enter credentials. SSO enhances user experience by reducing password fatigue and streamlining access, while also improving security by minimizing the risk of password reuse and credential theft. For large organizations with diverse application ecosystems, SSO simplifies identity management by centralizing authentication processes and enabling consistent enforcement of security policies.

To ensure scalability, identity architectures must support federated identity management. Federation establishes trust relationships between different identity providers, enabling users to authenticate with their home organization's credentials and access resources across multiple domains or organizations. This is particularly important for businesses that collaborate with external partners, suppliers, and customers, as it facilitates secure and seamless access without the need for managing multiple sets of credentials. Standard protocols such as SAML (Security Assertion Markup Language), OAuth, and OpenID Connect are commonly used to implement federated identity systems, ensuring interoperability and secure authentication across different platforms.

Multi-factor authentication (MFA) is another essential component of a scalable identity architecture. MFA enhances security by requiring users to provide multiple forms of verification, such as a password combined with a one-time code sent to a mobile device or biometric authentication like a fingerprint scan. As organizations grow and the number of users increases, implementing MFA helps protect against unauthorized access and reduces the risk of data breaches. Scalable identity architectures should support flexible MFA configurations, allowing organizations to tailor authentication requirements based on user roles, risk levels, and contextual factors.

Role-based access control (RBAC) and attribute-based access control (ABAC) are critical for managing permissions in a scalable identity architecture. RBAC assigns access rights based on predefined roles within the organization, simplifying the management of permissions as the number of users grows. ABAC provides more granular control by evaluating a combination of attributes, such as user identity, device, location, and time of access, to determine permissions. By implementing these access control models, organizations can ensure that users have the appropriate level of access based on their roles and responsibilities, reducing the risk of over-privileged accounts and unauthorized access.

Automation plays a vital role in building a scalable identity architecture. Manual processes for provisioning and de-provisioning user accounts, managing access rights, and conducting access reviews become increasingly cumbersome and error-prone as organizations grow. Automated identity governance solutions streamline these processes, ensuring that user identities and access rights are managed efficiently and consistently. Automation also supports compliance by maintaining detailed audit logs, enforcing policy adherence, and facilitating regular access reviews.

Scalable identity architectures must also address the growing complexity of device management. With the proliferation of mobile devices, Internet of Things (IoT) devices, and remote work environments, organizations need to manage a diverse array of endpoints. Identity and access management (IAM) systems should integrate with mobile device management (MDM) and endpoint detection and response (EDR) solutions to enforce security policies, monitor device activity, and ensure that only compliant devices can access corporate resources. This integration helps maintain security while supporting the flexibility and mobility required in modern work environments.

Cloud-native identity solutions offer significant advantages for scalability. Cloud-based IAM platforms provide elastic scalability, allowing organizations to adjust resources dynamically based on demand. This flexibility is particularly valuable for businesses experiencing rapid growth, seasonal fluctuations, or varying workloads. Cloud-native solutions also offer high availability and redundancy, ensuring that identity services remain operational even during hardware failures or network outages. By leveraging cloud infrastructure, organizations can reduce the costs and complexities associated with maintaining on-premises identity systems.

Security and compliance are paramount in scalable identity architectures. As organizations expand, they must ensure that their identity management practices comply with relevant regulations, such as the General Data Protection Regulation (GDPR), the California Consumer Privacy Act (CCPA), and industry-specific standards like the Health Insurance Portability and Accountability Act (HIPAA). Identity architectures should include robust data protection measures, such as encryption, secure storage of credentials, and regular security assessments. Additionally, IAM systems should support detailed logging and reporting to facilitate compliance audits and demonstrate adherence to regulatory requirements.

Monitoring and analytics are essential for maintaining the security and performance of scalable identity architectures. Continuous monitoring of user activities, authentication events, and access patterns helps detect anomalies and potential security threats in real time. Security Information and Event Management (SIEM) systems can aggregate and analyze logs from various sources, providing insights into identity-related risks and enabling proactive responses to incidents. Advanced analytics and machine learning algorithms can further enhance threat detection by identifying subtle patterns and deviations that may indicate malicious activity.

User experience is a critical consideration in scalable identity architecture. As the number of users and applications grows, it's important to ensure that identity management processes do not become cumbersome or intrusive. User-friendly interfaces, streamlined authentication workflows, and self-service capabilities contribute to a positive user experience, reducing the likelihood of security workarounds and increasing user satisfaction. For example, providing self-service portals for password resets, access requests, and profile management empowers users to manage their identities efficiently while reducing the burden on IT support teams.

Interoperability and integration are key to building a scalable identity architecture that supports diverse environments and evolving business needs. IAM systems should integrate seamlessly with existing IT infrastructure, cloud platforms, third-party applications, and emerging technologies. Open standards and APIs facilitate this integration, enabling organizations to adapt their identity architecture to new requirements and technologies without significant disruption. This flexibility ensures that the identity architecture remains agile and responsive to changing business landscapes.

Building a scalable identity architecture is not a one-time effort but an ongoing process that requires continuous improvement and adaptation. As organizations evolve, their identity management needs will change, necessitating regular reviews and updates to identity policies, processes, and technologies. Engaging stakeholders across the organization, including IT, security, compliance, and business units, ensures that identity strategies align with broader business objectives and address the needs of all users.

Ultimately, a scalable identity architecture is a strategic asset that supports organizational growth, enhances security, and improves operational efficiency. By investing in modern IAM solutions, adopting best practices, and fostering a culture of security and user empowerment, organizations can build identity architectures that meet the demands of today's digital world and position themselves for future success.

Identity Verification in E-Commerce and Online Services

In the rapidly expanding world of e-commerce and online services, identity verification has emerged as a critical component of secure transactions, fraud prevention, and customer trust. As consumers increasingly turn to digital platforms for shopping, banking, and accessing a wide array of services, businesses face the dual challenge of providing seamless, user-friendly experiences while ensuring that transactions are secure and legitimate. Identity verification processes help confirm that individuals are who they claim to be, mitigating the risks associated with identity theft, account takeover, and fraudulent activities. The ability to verify identities accurately and efficiently not only protects businesses from financial losses but also fosters confidence among consumers, which is essential for long-term success in the digital marketplace.

One of the primary reasons identity verification is so vital in e-commerce and online services is the rise of cybercrime. Fraudulent activities, such as credit card fraud, account takeovers, and phishing attacks, are pervasive threats that can result in significant financial losses for both businesses and consumers. Without robust identity verification processes in place, malicious actors can easily exploit vulnerabilities in online systems, leading to unauthorized transactions, data breaches, and compromised accounts. For example, an attacker might use stolen credentials to make unauthorized purchases on an e-commerce platform or gain access to sensitive financial information through a compromised online banking account. Effective identity verification serves as the first line of defense against such threats, ensuring that only legitimate users can access accounts and complete transactions.

The methods used for identity verification in e-commerce and online services have evolved significantly over the years. Traditionally, businesses relied on simple username and password combinations to authenticate users. However, as cyber threats have become more sophisticated, these basic methods are no longer sufficient. Passwords can be easily stolen, guessed, or cracked through brute-force attacks, and users often exacerbate the problem by choosing weak passwords or reusing the same credentials across multiple platforms. To address these vulnerabilities, businesses have adopted more advanced identity verification techniques that combine multiple layers of security.

Multi-factor authentication (MFA) is one of the most effective methods for enhancing identity verification. MFA requires users to provide two or more forms of verification before gaining access to their accounts. These factors typically include something the user knows (a password or PIN), something the user has (a smartphone or security token), and something the user is (biometric data such as a fingerprint or facial recognition). By requiring multiple forms of verification, MFA significantly reduces the likelihood of unauthorized access, even if one factor, such as a password, is compromised. For e-commerce platforms and online services, implementing MFA helps protect user accounts from unauthorized transactions and builds consumer trust by demonstrating a commitment to security.

Biometric authentication is another increasingly popular method for identity verification in online services. Biometric data, such as fingerprints, facial features, voice patterns, and iris scans, are unique to each individual and difficult to replicate, making them highly effective for verifying identities. Many smartphones and devices now come equipped with biometric sensors, allowing users to authenticate themselves quickly and securely without the need to remember complex passwords. In e-commerce, biometric authentication can streamline the checkout process, enabling users to complete purchases with a simple fingerprint scan or facial recognition, while ensuring that transactions are secure and legitimate.

In addition to MFA and biometric authentication, knowledge-based verification (KBV) is commonly used in e-commerce and online services. KBV involves asking users to answer security questions based on personal information, such as their mother's maiden name, the name of their first pet, or the street they grew up on. While KBV can add an extra layer of security, it is not foolproof. Much of the information used in KBV can be easily obtained through social engineering, data breaches, or public records, making it less reliable than other verification methods. As a result, businesses are increasingly moving away from KBV in favor of more secure and dynamic authentication techniques.

Document verification is another important aspect of identity verification in online services, particularly for platforms that require high levels of trust, such as financial services, online marketplaces, and gig economy platforms. Document verification involves users submitting government-issued identification, such as a passport, driver's license, or national ID card, which is then verified using automated systems or manual review. Advanced document verification solutions use technologies like optical character recognition (OCR), machine learning, and artificial intelligence to analyze the submitted documents for authenticity, checking for signs of tampering, forgery, or inconsistencies. This process helps ensure that users are who they claim to be and prevents fraudulent actors from creating fake accounts or engaging in illegal activities.

In e-commerce, identity verification also plays a critical role in preventing chargebacks and payment fraud. Chargebacks occur when a customer disputes a transaction, often claiming that it was unauthorized or that they did not receive the goods or services as promised. While chargebacks are intended to protect consumers from fraud, they can be costly for businesses, leading to financial losses, increased processing fees, and potential damage to merchant accounts. By implementing robust identity verification measures, such as address verification systems (AVS), card verification value (CVV) checks, and real-time fraud detection tools, businesses can reduce the risk of fraudulent transactions and minimize chargeback disputes.

Real-time fraud detection and risk-based authentication are advanced techniques that enhance identity verification in e-commerce and online services. These methods use machine learning algorithms and behavioral analytics to assess the risk of each transaction based on various factors, such as the user's location, device, transaction history, and behavior patterns. For example, if a user suddenly attempts to make a large purchase from an unfamiliar device or IP address, the system can flag the transaction as high-risk and prompt additional verification steps. Conversely, if the transaction aligns with the user's typical behavior, the system can streamline the process, allowing for a frictionless experience. This dynamic approach to identity verification balances security with user convenience, providing a seamless experience while protecting against fraud.

The rise of mobile commerce (m-commerce) has introduced new challenges and opportunities for identity verification. As more consumers use smartphones and tablets to shop online, businesses must ensure that their identity verification processes are optimized for mobile devices. This includes implementing mobile-friendly authentication methods, such as biometric verification, SMS-based one-time passwords (OTPs), and app-based authentication tools. Mobile identity verification solutions must also account for the unique security risks associated with mobile devices, such as SIM card swapping, device theft, and malware. By adopting mobile-centric identity verification strategies, businesses can provide secure and convenient experiences for their mobile customers.

Privacy and data protection are critical considerations in identity verification for e-commerce and online services. Consumers are increasingly concerned about how their personal information is collected, stored, and used by businesses. Regulations such as the General Data Protection Regulation (GDPR) and the California Consumer Privacy Act (CCPA) impose strict requirements on data protection and user consent, mandating that businesses implement transparent and secure identity verification practices. This includes using encryption to protect sensitive data, minimizing data collection to only what is necessary, and providing users with control over their personal information. By prioritizing privacy and compliance, businesses can build trust with their customers and differentiate themselves in a competitive marketplace.

The future of identity verification in e-commerce and online services is likely to be shaped by emerging technologies and evolving consumer expectations. Decentralized identity (DID) frameworks, which leverage blockchain technology to give users control over their digital identities, offer promising solutions for secure and privacy-respecting identity verification. In a decentralized identity model, users store their credentials in digital wallets and share only the necessary information with service providers, reducing the risk of data breaches and identity theft. Additionally, advancements in artificial intelligence and machine learning will continue to enhance fraud detection and identity verification processes, making them more accurate, efficient, and user-friendly.

In conclusion, identity verification is a cornerstone of secure and successful e-commerce and online services. By adopting advanced authentication methods, leveraging emerging technologies, and prioritizing privacy and user experience, businesses can protect themselves from fraud, build customer trust, and thrive in the digital marketplace. As the landscape of online transactions continues to evolve, robust identity verification will remain essential for ensuring the integrity and security of digital interactions.

Community and Open Source Contributions to Identity Solutions

The evolution of digital identity management has been significantly influenced by contributions from the open-source community and collaborative projects. As organizations increasingly rely on digital platforms for authentication, authorization, and access control, the demand for flexible, scalable, and secure identity solutions has grown. Open-source initiatives have stepped in to meet this demand, offering innovative tools, frameworks, and protocols that drive the development of modern identity systems. The collaborative nature of open-source projects fosters rapid innovation, transparency, and adaptability, making them a cornerstone in the identity management landscape.

Open-source contributions to identity solutions span a wide range of technologies, from authentication protocols and access management frameworks to comprehensive identity governance platforms. One of the key advantages of open-source identity solutions is their transparency. Unlike proprietary systems, which often operate as black boxes, open-source projects allow organizations to inspect, modify, and customize the source code to meet their specific needs. This transparency not only enhances security by enabling thorough code audits but also builds trust within the community, as users can verify that the software operates as intended.

A prominent example of open-source influence in identity management is the development and adoption of authentication protocols such as OAuth 2.0 and OpenID Connect. OAuth 2.0, an open standard for authorization, enables third-party applications to access user resources without exposing credentials. OpenID Connect, built on top of OAuth 2.0, provides an identity layer that facilitates secure user authentication across different platforms. These protocols have become foundational to modern identity solutions, enabling secure and seamless single sign-on (SSO) experiences across a multitude of applications and services. Their open nature has encouraged widespread adoption and continuous improvement by developers and organizations worldwide.

Another significant contribution from the open-source community is the creation of identity and access management (IAM) frameworks that offer robust, scalable, and customizable solutions. Projects like Keycloak, an open-source identity and access management solution developed by Red Hat, provide features such as SSO, user federation, and support for standard protocols like SAML and OpenID Connect. Keycloak allows organizations to manage user identities, roles, and permissions with ease, while its extensibility ensures that it can be tailored to meet unique business requirements. The active community surrounding Keycloak contributes to its continuous enhancement, ensuring that it remains up-to-date with the latest security standards and best practices.

Similarly, Apache Syncope is another open-source project that exemplifies community-driven innovation in identity management. As an identity governance and administration (IGA) platform, Syncope offers capabilities for managing digital identities, roles, entitlements, and compliance. It provides a centralized system for provisioning and de-provisioning user accounts across diverse IT environments, streamlining identity lifecycle management. The collaborative development model of Syncope ensures that it evolves in response to real-world challenges and user feedback, making it a reliable and adaptable solution for organizations of all sizes.

The open-source community has also played a crucial role in advancing identity federation and single sign-on solutions. Shibboleth, an open-source project that implements SAML-based SSO, enables organizations to establish federated identity systems that allow users to access resources across different institutions using a single set of credentials. This is particularly valuable in academic and research environments, where collaboration across institutions is common. The

Shibboleth Consortium, which oversees the project, exemplifies how community governance and collective expertise can drive the development of secure and interoperable identity solutions.

In addition to providing technical solutions, open-source projects foster a culture of collaboration, knowledge sharing, and continuous learning within the identity management community. Forums, mailing lists, and online communities serve as platforms for developers, security professionals, and organizations to share insights, troubleshoot issues, and contribute to the evolution of identity technologies. This collaborative environment accelerates the development of new features, enhances security through peer review, and ensures that identity solutions remain responsive to emerging threats and technological advancements.

The role of open standards organizations, such as the OpenID Foundation and the Internet Engineering Task Force (IETF), further illustrates the impact of community contributions on identity solutions. These organizations bring together stakeholders from diverse backgrounds to develop and maintain open standards that underpin secure and interoperable identity systems. By fostering collaboration among industry leaders, academics, and independent developers, open standards organizations ensure that identity protocols and frameworks are robust, scalable, and widely adopted.

Open-source contributions to identity solutions are not limited to software development; they also encompass educational resources, best practices, and security guidelines. Projects like OWASP (Open Web Application Security Project) provide invaluable resources for securing identity systems, including guidelines for implementing secure authentication, managing credentials, and mitigating common vulnerabilities. The OWASP Top Ten, a widely recognized list of critical web application security risks, serves as a reference for developers and security professionals seeking to build secure identity solutions.

The flexibility and adaptability of open-source identity solutions make them particularly well-suited for addressing the diverse needs of organizations across different industries and regions. For example, in the healthcare sector, open-source identity solutions enable secure access to electronic health records (EHRs) and support compliance with regulations such as the Health Insurance Portability and Accountability Act (HIPAA). In the financial sector, open-source IAM frameworks facilitate secure customer authentication and support compliance with regulations like the Payment Card Industry Data Security Standard (PCI DSS). The ability to customize and extend open-source solutions ensures that they can meet the specific requirements of various regulatory environments and industry standards.

The integration of emerging technologies into open-source identity solutions further highlights the dynamic nature of community contributions. Projects that leverage blockchain technology for decentralized identity management, such as Hyperledger Indy and Sovrin, demonstrate how open-source initiatives are pushing the boundaries of traditional identity paradigms. Decentralized identity frameworks empower individuals to own and control their digital identities, enhancing privacy and security while reducing reliance on centralized identity providers. The open-source model ensures that these innovative solutions remain transparent, interoperable, and accessible to a broad audience.

Despite the many advantages of open-source identity solutions, organizations must also be mindful of potential challenges. Ensuring the security and integrity of open-source software requires diligent code review, regular updates, and active participation in the community. Organizations must also evaluate the maturity and support structures of open-source projects to ensure that they align with their operational and security requirements. However, the collaborative nature of open-source development often results in rapid identification and resolution of security vulnerabilities, making open-source solutions a viable and secure choice for many organizations.

The future of identity management will continue to be shaped by the contributions of the open-source community. As digital identity becomes increasingly central to secure online interactions, the demand for innovative, flexible, and transparent identity solutions will grow. Open-source projects will play a pivotal role in meeting this demand, driving the development of new technologies, protocols, and best practices that ensure secure and seamless identity experiences.

In summary, the open-source community has had a profound impact on the development of identity solutions, offering transparent, adaptable, and secure tools that meet the diverse needs of modern organizations. Through collaborative development, knowledge sharing, and adherence to open standards, open-source initiatives have driven innovation and enhanced the security of digital identity systems. As the landscape of identity management continues to evolve, the contributions of the open-source community will remain essential in shaping the future of secure, scalable, and user-centric identity solutions.

The Path Forward: Innovating in Identity Authentication and Authorization

As the digital world continues to expand and evolve, the challenges and demands surrounding identity authentication and authorization are becoming increasingly complex. With the proliferation of cloud computing, mobile devices, the Internet of Things (IoT), and remote workforces, securing digital identities has never been more critical. Cyber threats grow in sophistication, and the traditional methods of managing identities and access are no longer sufficient to protect sensitive information and ensure seamless user experiences. To stay ahead, organizations must embrace innovation in identity authentication and authorization, adopting new technologies and strategies that enhance security, improve user convenience, and support the dynamic needs of modern digital environments.

One of the key drivers of innovation in identity authentication is the shift from static, password-based systems to more dynamic and secure methods. Passwords, long the cornerstone of digital security, are increasingly recognized as a weak link in identity management. They are prone to being forgotten, reused, or stolen through phishing attacks, credential stuffing, and data breaches. As a result, the industry is moving toward passwordless authentication methods, which offer both improved security and user convenience. Technologies such as biometrics, hardware security tokens, and one-time passcodes (OTPs) are becoming more prevalent, allowing users to authenticate without relying on traditional passwords. Biometric authentication, in particular, leverages unique physical characteristics like fingerprints, facial recognition, and voice patterns to verify identity, providing a highly secure and user-friendly alternative.

In addition to passwordless authentication, multi-factor authentication (MFA) continues to evolve as a cornerstone of secure identity verification. While MFA is already widely adopted, innovations are making it more adaptive and intelligent. Risk-based or adaptive authentication analyzes contextual factors, such as user location, device, and behavior patterns, to assess the risk level of each login attempt. If the system detects an anomaly—such as a login from an unfamiliar device or an unusual geographic location—it can trigger additional verification steps. Conversely, if the login attempt aligns with the user's normal behavior, the system may streamline the authentication process, reducing friction. This balance of security and usability is critical for maintaining user engagement while protecting against threats.

Decentralized identity is another groundbreaking innovation shaping the future of identity authentication and authorization. Traditional identity systems rely on centralized authorities to manage and verify identities, creating single points of failure and raising concerns about privacy and data security. Decentralized identity frameworks, often built on blockchain technology, shift control from centralized entities to individuals. In this model, users own and manage their digital identities, storing credentials in secure digital wallets and sharing only the necessary information with service providers. This approach enhances privacy, reduces the risk of data breaches, and empowers users to have greater control over their personal information. Projects like Microsoft's Identity Overlay Network (ION) and the Sovrin Network exemplify how decentralized identity is transforming the landscape of digital authentication.

The integration of artificial intelligence (AI) and machine learning (ML) into identity authentication and authorization systems is also driving significant innovation. AI and ML algorithms can analyze vast amounts of data to detect patterns and anomalies that may indicate security threats, such as unauthorized access attempts or credential misuse. These technologies enable real-time threat detection and automated responses, enhancing the security of identity systems. For example, AI-driven systems can flag suspicious login attempts based on unusual behavior and prompt additional verification steps, or they can automatically lock accounts when potential breaches are detected. By continuously learning and adapting to new threats, AI and ML enhance the resilience and effectiveness of identity management solutions.

The rise of the Internet of Things (IoT) presents both opportunities and challenges for identity authentication and authorization. As more devices become interconnected, managing the identities and access permissions of these devices becomes increasingly complex. Traditional identity management systems are not designed to handle the sheer volume and diversity of IoT devices, many of which have limited processing power and security capabilities. Innovations in IoT identity management focus on lightweight authentication protocols, secure device provisioning, and automated access control mechanisms that can scale to accommodate millions of devices. Ensuring the security and integrity of IoT ecosystems requires robust identity solutions that can authenticate devices, manage permissions, and detect anomalies in device behavior.

Federated identity management is evolving to support more seamless and secure interactions across different organizations and platforms. Federated identity allows users to authenticate once and access multiple systems across organizational boundaries, using a single set of credentials. Innovations in this space focus on enhancing interoperability, improving security protocols, and expanding the use of federated identity in new contexts, such as cross-border transactions and multi-cloud environments. Standardized protocols like SAML, OAuth, and OpenID Connect continue to evolve, enabling more flexible and secure federated identity solutions that support diverse use cases and industries.

The concept of zero trust architecture (ZTA) is revolutionizing the way organizations approach identity authentication and authorization. In a zero trust model, no user or device is inherently trusted, regardless of whether they are inside or outside the corporate network. Instead, every access request is continuously verified based on multiple factors, including user identity, device health, location, and behavior. This approach minimizes the risk of unauthorized access and lateral movement within the network, providing a more robust security posture. Innovations in zero trust identity management focus on integrating identity verification with continuous monitoring and dynamic access controls, ensuring that trust is constantly evaluated and adjusted based on real-time data.

Cloud-based identity and access management (IAM) solutions are also driving innovation in the field. As organizations increasingly migrate to cloud environments, they require identity solutions that are scalable, flexible, and capable of supporting hybrid and multi-cloud architectures. Cloud IAM platforms offer centralized control over identity management, enabling organizations to manage user identities, access permissions, and security policies across diverse environments from a single interface. These solutions often include advanced features such as automated provisioning, real-time access monitoring, and integration with other cloud services, streamlining identity management and enhancing security.

Privacy-enhancing technologies (PETs) are becoming integral to the future of identity authentication and authorization. As consumers and regulators demand greater transparency and control over personal data, organizations must find ways to authenticate and authorize users without compromising privacy. Techniques such as zero-knowledge proofs, homomorphic encryption, and differential privacy enable secure identity verification while minimizing the exposure of sensitive information. For example, zero-knowledge proofs allow one party to prove their identity to another without revealing any additional information, preserving privacy while ensuring security. The integration of PETs into identity systems helps organizations comply with data protection regulations and build trust with users.

The role of open standards and open-source contributions in identity innovation cannot be overstated. Open standards ensure interoperability between different identity systems and foster collaboration across industries. Organizations like the OpenID Foundation, the Fast Identity Online (FIDO) Alliance, and the World Wide Web Consortium (W3C) play crucial roles in developing and maintaining standards that drive innovation in identity authentication and authorization. Open-source projects, such as Keycloak, Gluu, and ForgeRock, provide flexible, transparent, and customizable identity solutions that can be adapted to meet specific organizational needs.

The collaborative nature of open-source development accelerates the adoption of new technologies and ensures that identity solutions remain secure, reliable, and aligned with industry best practices.

As identity authentication and authorization continue to evolve, the focus is increasingly on user-centric solutions that balance security with convenience. The goal is to create identity systems that are not only secure but also intuitive and seamless for users. This involves reducing friction in the authentication process, providing consistent experiences across devices and platforms, and empowering users with greater control over their digital identities. Innovations in user experience design, biometric authentication, and adaptive authentication contribute to creating identity systems that meet these goals, enhancing both security and user satisfaction.

The future of identity authentication and authorization is being shaped by a combination of technological advancements, regulatory changes, and evolving user expectations. Organizations that embrace innovation in identity management will be better positioned to protect their digital assets, comply with regulatory requirements, and deliver exceptional user experiences. By leveraging emerging technologies, adopting open standards, and fostering a culture of continuous improvement, organizations can navigate the complexities of the digital landscape and build resilient, future-proof identity systems that support their long-term success.